SECRETS OF THE SOES BANDIT

SECRETS OF THE SOES BANDIT

The Original Electronic Trader Reveals His Battle-Tested Trading Techniques

HARVEY HOUTKIN
WITH DAVID WALDMAN

McGraw-Hill
New York • San Francisco • Washington, D.C. • Auckland
Bogotá • Caracas • Lisbon • London • Madrid • Mexico City
Milan • Montreal • New Delhi • San Juan • Singapore
Sydney • Tokyo • Toronto

Library of Congress Cataloging-in-Publication Data

Houtkin, Harvey I.
    Secrets of the SOES bandit / by Harvey Houtkin with David Waldman.
        p. cm.
    ISBN 0-07-030577-3
    1. Electronic trading of securities. I. Waldman, David.
II. Title.
HG4515.95.H678   1998
332.64'0285—dc21   98-27619
                                                                                            CIP

McGraw-Hill

A Division of The McGraw·Hill Companies

  2 3 4 5 6 7 8 9 0   DOC/DOC   9 0 4 3 2 1 0 9

ISBN 0-07-030577-3

*The sponsoring editor for this book was Stephen Isaacs, the editing
supervisor was Caroline Levine, and the production supervisor was
Suzanne Rapcavage. It was set in Fairfield per the NBF specs by
Patricia Caruso and Dennis Smith of McGraw-Hill's Professional
Book Group composition unit, Hightstown, N.J.*

Printed and bound by R. R. Donnelley & Sons Company.

The opinions expressed herein are those of the authors. There can be
no guarantee of trading or financial success.

Direct Access Electronic Trading via a proper trading system operated by a brokerage firm (formerly called SOES trading) is not for
everyone. It requires training, drive, stamina, discipline, memory,
some intelligence, and the ability to allocate financial resources
which you can afford to lose and are not needed for other purposes.

Because Direct Access Electronic Trading often utilizes margin, it
is possible that potential losses may exceed the amount invested.

To both our families, with love and appreciation

On Wall Street, there once was a buttonwood tree, tall, old, now legendary. Under it the first stocks were said to have been traded in the late 1700s. In the 1880s, J. Pierpont Morgan, that age's quintessential industrialist, treated stocks solely as the domain of financiers. In the 1900s, Charles Merrill's brokers took Wall Street to Main Street, looking for customers among ordinary folk. Two decades ago, Charles Schwab launched the discount brokerage business, inviting Main Street to bypass Merrill's hefty commissions. At the beginning of the 1990s, Harvey Houtkin invited people to circumvent brokers entirely: Pull up a chair and plug in to the game yourself.

STEVE FISHMAN
"Brokers wild,"
Details, October 1997

CONTENTS

CHAPTER SIX. HOW TO TRADE   77

PREFACE

In the last few years a significant number of industrywide entry barriers to profitable trading have disappeared and the average person is no longer deprived of crucial privileges previously enjoyed by Wall Street insiders exclusively. *Secrets of the SOES Bandit* will reveal the manner in which market insiders dealt with the public in the past and will show you how to benefit from newly enacted regulatory changes.

After generations of insider self-regulatory dereliction, a new environment has been created in which anyone with the financial ability, intelligence, and desire can compete effectively in the fabulous world of Wall Street. No longer does the financial community dictate the terms of your participation.

Advances in technology coupled with regulatory changes have empowered the public investor and trader. Trading is now a mainstream occupational alternative, and the benefits and lifestyle it can provide are available to all who qualify.

Since the publication of my last book in the spring of 1995, an accelerated revolution has changed totally the face of the markets in general and the Nasdaq in particular. Regulatory change has benefited the little guy, and the public is finally getting a fair shot at the Wall Street game as Nasdaq's computerized Small Order Execution System (SOES) has proved to be the catalyst for the new market climate. Market maker resistance has turned into reluctant acceptance of Direct Access Electronic Trading (DAET), my advanced trading system through which traders have instant market access to SOES, DOT (the NYSE routing system), and an entire generation of electronic communications networks

(ECNs). As a result, individuals can now trade for their own accounts as a mainstream endeavor.

This book provides my overview of the way major trading markets have been operating after the revolution and what it means for you. Furthermore, I will discuss the art of trading and impart insightful trading advice and tips, which put you in control of the way in which your orders will interact in the market. I will also expose in layman's terms those secrets that your broker never tells you or may not even be aware of. I will show how markets will operate in the future, after reviewing the lessons learned from the past.

Secrets of the SOES Bandit will reveal market practices previously undisclosed by an industry that has preferred dealing with an "informationless" public unaware of the "professional courtesies" and customs and practices etched in the interdealer behavior code. For example, until recently even the NYSE ticker tape seen on national business TV was delayed arbitrarily for 15 minutes. As of this writing, Nasdaq continues to delay the dissemination of its trading quotes for no ethical or explainable reason. If a plane crashed in your front yard, would you wait 15 minutes to disclose the news?

Hundreds of millions of dollars are being paid currently by leading brokerage firms as restitution for unethical trading practices involving price fixing and collusion to defraud the public. The manner in which the brokerage community has treated the public for years is rapidly coming to an end because of significant changes in the regulatory environment and a shift in public perception concerning rights of investors.

Many people are reluctant to accept change because they have become comfortable with the status quo. But those who can embrace change and turn it to their advantage will prove to be the most successful. They will reap the benefit of getting in early and prospering before the change becomes public domain.

By exploring this book in detail you can come away with enough knowledge to evaluate Direct Access Electronic Trading and decide whether this opportunity is appropriate for you. Trading has captured the imagination not only of the investment and trading communities but also a large segment of the general investing public. The reasons are obvious:

- The public wants to be better informed about their investments in particular and market opportunity in general.
- The NASD has agreed to abolish collusive price action by market makers who maintain artificially wide spreads in the prices of securities traded on Nasdaq.
- Investors and traders love the electronic changes that allow them to profit from new opportunities and compete equally with other market participants.
- A new cottage industry, Direct Access Electronic Trading, has developed with few barriers to entry.
- The secrets of market reality are being exposed, and new traders are being instructed in the art of turning trading into a mainstream occupation.
- People have become far more aware of the importance of order execution, including price, speed of execution, and the "real" cost of trading.
- Informed investors demand competitive brokerage commissions and an understanding of the services rendered and the true cost thereof.

Direct Access Electronic Trading has become an issue of national and international importance because it pierces to the heart of the way markets operate and should operate. SOES was the catalyst for regulatory change that has created the environment for Direct Access Electronic Trading.

Direct Access Electronic Trading is the level playing field I have striven so hard to create. DAET is the magic bullet that does away with the old way of doing business and enhances your ability to profit.

Direct Access Electronic Trading is the opportunity of a lifetime. It allows the investor to obtain all the information necessary to work for the best execution of an order at a low, real transaction fee. You do not want your broker as your partner in your stock trades. A $100-a-share stock should not cost more to buy than a $10-a-share stock.

Harvey Houtkin
with *David Waldman*

Any questions or comments may be directed to the authors' e-mail addresses:
harvey@attain.com   david@attain.com

WHAT IS DIRECT ACCESS ELECTRONIC TRADING AND SOES TRADING?

THE SOES "BANDIT"

You've read about me and my SOES trading techniques in *Fortune, Time, Forbes, Business Week,* the *New York Times, London Financial Times,* the *Los Angeles Times,* the *Wall Street Journal,* and virtually every other legitimate publication covering Wall Street or business news. You've seen me interviewed on television on shows such as *Wall Street Journal Report,* and on CNN, WWOR, CNBC, and even the BBC (the British Broadcasting Corporation). I have also been the cohost of the morning business news of CNBC. Why all the interest? Well, some people claim I have found the key to the vault— *Direct Access Electronic Trading* (DAET). This is not just any trading, but predominantly day trading on Nasdaq and other listed securities utilizing an advanced trading system through which traders have instant market access to Nasdaq's computerized *Small Order Execution System* (SOES), DOT (the NYSE routing system to trade listed securities), and an entire generation of existing and emerging electronic communications networks (ECNs).

Your DAET system should be feature-rich, with enticing bells and whistles, which provide all the information you will need to formulate a trading decision and have your trade executed. In effect, you will have many of the advantages of owning a seat on an exchange without the need to buy a seat or pay monthly membership dues.

Don't call me a SOES bandit. In fact, all I am is an average guy trying to make a dollar in the market utilizing the electronics of today. I prefer being called a DAET trader.

It may seem unusual for someone to have worn the "bandit" badge with pride, but strange things happen in the crazy world of Wall Street. "Bandit," "shark," "electronic highwayman," and "roach" are just a few of the labels bestowed on me by my market-making peers on Wall Street. Animosity toward my trading activities by the Nasdaq market-making community and the National Association of Securities Dealers (NASD), itself is probably unprecedented in the U.S. financial markets.

Why the furor? It's quite obvious—if I can cause this much outrage and denunciation from big, powerful market-making firms, I must be doing something very right. Why else would some of the most successful traders, utilizing billions of dollars in capital—traders having every conceivable advantage, traders who deal with every major institution—feel threatened by a small group of individuals who are trading small quantities of "high-cap" Nasdaq securities at current quoted prices? The answer to this question spells big trouble for Wall Street traders and unlimited opportunity for individual public day traders.

ELECTRONIC DAY TRADING

Day trading has been an honorable, rewarding, and legitimate activity since financial markets began trading. Wall Street professionals who participate in day trading activities, such as dealers, speculators, traders, market makers, locals, floor traders, and specialists, are usually held in high regard, and the successful participants are usually the subject of great admiration and envy.

The securities industry—securities marketplaces and exchanges for stocks, bonds, commodities, options, etc.—has always chosen to have rules and regulations that put the individual investor or trader at a significant disadvantage to the "pro." Besides not knowing the *spread* (the difference between bid and ask prices), which is the most obvious disadvantage, poor access to the "real" market made day trading almost impossible for the average person. Other obstacles included high direct and indirect commission costs and *lack of access* to order execution (real-time quotations and services).

Put all these obstacles together and the chances of succeeding as a public day trader were slim to none.

Why become a day trader? Simply put, there is no activity more exciting, more exhilarating, and potentially more rewarding. Day traders trade *flat*—that is, they don't usually take home overnight positions in securities. Therefore, at 4 p.m., the close of trading, their day is truly over—no worries or stress until the next day they wish to day trade. They're off weekends and holidays and may take a vacation any time they choose. Certainly there is risk, intensity, and stress during trading hours—but only during trading hours. And those hours go by quickly. Many of my associates curse the long weekends that keep them away from trading. Day trading is so exhilarating that it can become almost addictive.

A day trader is usually held in high regard by peers. I would say a successful day trader is held in the same high regard as professionals, such as doctors, lawyers, and dentists. However, unlike other professions, day trading offers unlimited earnings potential. The earnings potential has been written about in major national publications such as, *Time, Forbes, Business Week, Barron's,* and the *New York Times,* and so I won't discuss it here. Besides, if I disclosed the results you probably wouldn't believe them anyway. Suffice it to say that many of my customers who were formerly unemployed or underemployed now park their Mercedes in their luxury home's garage. In many cases, they earn incomes, equal to or better than those of the professionals mentioned above. Of course, not everyone is successful. There are a percentage of the people who lose money, but they lose because they *stopped* day trading, lost their discipline, and, for one reason or another, became "investors."

SUCCESSFUL TRADING IS THE KEY

If you meet the parameters set forth in this book and follow the outlined strategies carefully, your probability of success will be exceptionally high. No matter what your sex is, or your age, or your race or nationality, or your educational level, you can become a successful SOES/DAET trader. I have trained machinists, beauticians, house painters, plumbers, bookkeepers, students, immigrants, retirees, doctors, lawyers, business owners, and others to trade. There are no defined criteria about educational background or work experience.

My techniques utilizing SOES, SelectNet, and now the ECNs have been so successful for nearly a decade that the market makers and the NASD have done everything in their power to reduce the effectiveness or eliminate these systems. Why? Because these systems legitimize the way securities are traded and level the playing field. However, recent independent studies, independent investigations by the SEC and the Justice Department, class-action lawsuits naming almost every major market-making firm, the forced reorganization of the NASD, and the revision of numerous trading rules in favor of the public customer have turned the tide by opening DAET opportunities for everyone.

Unlike other business opportunities, day trading requires no large illiquid capital investment. No up-front buy-in money need be spent, as it would be if you were acquiring a franchise or opening other types of business ventures. Capital is needed for margin purposes only. Naturally, if you trade poorly, your capital will be reduced. But Direct Access Electronic Traders have their capital back at the end of every day plus or minus their profit or loss for the day. This phenomenon makes DAET a most attractive opportunity for the qualified individual.

How many businesses can you liquidate for cash at fair market value every day and reenter whenever you choose, if you choose? What other business activity has an unlimited upside and very controllable downside? What business activity can be expanded or reduced at will? What business activity has the well-documented success of Direct Access Electronic Day Trading?

Day trading is *not* investing. It is a career. Your work is grinding out trading profits, and the reward is high earnings for the successful individual. This book will try to explain the criteria necessary for success, including "personality types," capital requirements, and all other relevant factors. This book is a primer for Direct Access Electronic Trading utilizing high-powered electronic trade execution systems that combine ECNs and various electronic trading mechanisms. After you study this book and decide trading is for you, you will be in a position to prosper beyond your most optimistic expectations.

If you are unhappy in your current field of endeavor, this book will offer you a window of opportunity you might not have thought existed. If you are currently active in the market, this book may cause you to alter your approach to trading and learn to trade far more successfully while enjoying every minute of it.

SOES

SOES was created by Nasdaq for the instantaneous and automatic execution of small orders. When coupled with the alternative trading markets available on ECNs, it is the most effective way for the small market player to access the Nasdaq market. While SOES coupled with the ECNs is presently, in my opinion, the most effective DAET mechanism, there are other *order routing* but not *order execution* systems utilized by virtually every stock exchange.

The existence of SOES, SelectNet, and the ECNs has eliminated significant advantages enjoyed for years by the market-making community. They enable the average person to get an "honest" (as described by the head of the NASD himself), immediate, legitimate execution and to bid and offer shares in between the spread to achieve better prices. The individual day trader can now have his or her orders receive virtually the same visibility as that of the market makers. Most importantly, it gives the individual the ability to have an order executed in a matter of split seconds.

DAET

DAET is essentially what most people once called SOES trading, but with added features and benefits. With the techniques and technology I have been developing and utilizing for almost a decade, DAET enables the astute, disciplined trader to prosper far more than imagined.

Day trading is an old and honorable means of trading in which the participant holds a position in a security for only a short period of time in order to benefit (it is hoped) from moment-to-moment price movements. Traders using DAET can act like floor traders or "locals" on any exchange floor in order to maintain liquidity in the market. But one great advantage to DAET is that you don't have to stand on your feet in the pit all day and shout at strangers who are shouting at you.

DAET, utilizing Nasdaq Level II quotes and information from SelectNet and the ECNs, makes the average individual as well informed on prevailing market conditions as the market maker. The Level II screens show "real" current prices in the process of changing, allowing more astute decision making. In conjunction with a broker-dealer having DAET order entry ability, it allows access to the market and immediate entry into a fast-moving situation. DAET puts you in control of your trading environment and allows you to "work" your own order.

A Direct Access Electronic Trader is essentially a twenty-first-century tape trader. How many times have you seen people sitting in a boardroom at a brokerage firm watching prices coming across a ticker tape? The ticker tape is the trader's primary source of trading ideas. As the symbols and prices float across the tape, occasionally someone will walk over to a broker and hand the broker an order based on something the client has identified on the tape. The broker will write up the order and pass it on to a Teletype operator or other input staff person, who will then send it to the floor of the appropriate exchange or to a Nasdaq order entry clerk for execution. In a few minutes the customer will receive an execution showing either the number of shares and price or a "nothing done," indicating the order did not get executed.

This type of delay is intolerable to the DAET trader. When a DAET trader enters an order, the trader expects it to be completed instantaneously. This is the amount of time a typical order executed through a first-class trading system should take to be executed—no ifs, ands, or buts. The DAET trader, for better or worse, always has hands-on control over his or her securities positions.

DAET involves intensive tape watching, but not in the conventional sense. Due to the rules of the Nasdaq market, all market makers in a particular stock electronically publish their current quotations on the Level II screen. Each quotation posted by a market-making dealer in a Nasdaq stock must contain the bid price (the price at which the dealer is willing to purchase shares), the offered price (the price at which the dealer is willing to sell shares), and the minimum stated size (usually 1000 shares) at which the stock must trade.

Your computerized access trading system should be the latest-generation, most effective, and most advanced medium for DAET because, among other reasons, it will give you superfast access to the other computer systems necessary to enable you to directly compete in the marketplace. You shouldn't skimp on the cost of a system. Get one that provides the best available information of vital need to DAET and access to Nasdaq and listed markets.

NASDAQ LEVEL II DAY TRADING SCREEN

Chart 1-1 shows a Nasdaq Level II screen with some of the features available to traders on a typical DAET computer screen.

The Ticker. The TICKER at the top left corner shows those stocks the trader desires to see, and identifies market makers who have changed the inside price (color-coded in real life

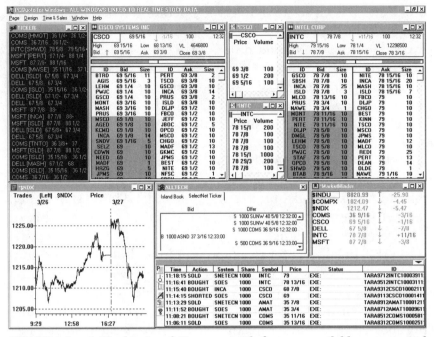

CHART 1-1. A Nasdaq Level II screen with features available on a typical DAET system.

with green indicating an uptick and red indicating a downtick). The TICKER can be customized to allow the trader to select those stocks the trader desires to watch.

Streaming Data. Each of the information boxes streams data to the trader. The window to the right of the TICKER is a MARKET MAKER window. Each of the windows dynamically refreshes with real-time stock data. Windows relating to a stock can easily be linked. The CSCO MARKET MAKER window is linked to the CSCO TIME OF SALE chart next to it.

The NASD Level I Screen. The top three lines of each MARKET MAKER window display the Nasdaq Level I screen, which is the only information that most brokers are normally allowed to see. The top line displays the name of the security, the last sale, an arrow to show whether that last sale was up or down and the amount of increase or decrease for the day, the order size, and the time of the last sale. The middle line of the Level I screen presents the Daily High, Low, and Volume of shares. The third line is the current Bid, Ask, and Yesterday's closing price.

The Ribbon.   A thin ribbon divides the relatively small portion of the NASD Level I information (shown on top of the ribbon) from the majority of the Level II information (directly below the ribbon). The ribbon looks like an armed services military ribbon with different colors running in a horizontal spectrum. The different colors demonstrate the depth of the market-maker quotes at every price, from highest to lowest (running from the center bar of the ribbon). The ribbon is a horizontal picture of the depth of the market which is vertically displayed on each MARKET MAKER screen.

The MARKET MAKER Window.   Chart 1-1 has one open MARKET MAKER window for Cisco Systems, Inc., and a second MARKET MAKER window open for Intel Corp. Each of these windows represents a Nasdaq Level II screen. The striated gray colors on each MARKET MAKER window (shown in vivid color on the real computer screen) represent different market-maker price levels. These price levels change as the ticker price changes. Prices (and colors) in the MARKET MAKER window will move up or down to reflect market direction.

Graphs.   The graph in the lower left-hand quadrant of the screen shows the Nasdaq 100 index for March 26 and for part of March 27. The time at the bottom is shown in military time. Your day trading system will be able to compile any chart or charts you require in relatively short order. It will also superimpose one chart upon another from a bundle of charts and time frames available for you to chose from. You will probably run out of important indexes before the quote program runs out of available charts. Important indexes that you can turn into graphic form include the Nasdaq composite index ($COMPX), the Nasdaq 100 index ($NDX), the U.S. 30-year Treasury bond future index (/USH8), and the S&P 500 cash index ($SPX). You can also chart the price of any stock and compare the stock's performance with any relevant index.

ALL TECH Window.   The ALL TECH window is sandwiched into the middle of Chart 1-1. This invaluable tool shows traders the Island Book and the SelectNet Ticker. The Island Book displays current trades on the Island ECN. The SelectNet Ticker displays the most recent trades on SelectNet. Both these tickers show actual executions and not amorphous dealer quotes which may never have printed at the quoted prices. There is a great difference between quotes and trades. My quoted price for selling my house may be $500,000. There may be several bigger, better houses on my block that recently sold for half that quoted price. See the difference?

MarketMinder Window.   The right-hand middle box is the MarketMinder window. This informs you of prices in all markets and stocks that you deem meaningful. I call this box the "Christmas tree" because the indicators are green or red. When all the indicators are green, every indicator is going up and thus the markets are going up. When all the indicators are red, the markets are going down.

Status Box.   The Status box is on the right side of the bottom row of Chart 1-1. It provides a running tally of the status of every trade you have executed or tried to execute for a particular day. It will also track your open positions by constantly popping them to the top line in this window. For example, the top line of the Status box shows that at 11:18:15 hours, the trader sold on SelectNet 1000 shares of INTC (Intel Corp.) at a price of $79 per share, status EXE (executed) with an identifying number of TARA9712INTC10003911. The identifier earmarks each trade so that no trade will be lost.

ADVANTAGES OF DAET TRADING

FINANCIAL INDUSTRY IMPEDIMENTS TO DAET

While it is true that it makes little difference what you trade as long as you trade it successfully, your ability to trade successfully can vary greatly depending on the arena in which you operate and the number of impediments you face. The securities industry spent many decades developing an environment that gives innumerable advantages to the industry participants (the pros). Unless the individual Direct Access Electronic Trader can also obtain certain of the advantages enjoyed by industry insiders, chances of success will be minimal.

Some of the industry's advantages are quite obvious, while others, although very real, are barely noticeable. The biggest obvious advantage of the professional market maker, and obstacle to the day trader, is the *spread*. The spread is the difference between the bid price (the price at which an individual can sell) and the offered or asked price (the price at which an individual can buy). The spread represents the market maker's reward for taking risk in a transaction. The fact that a market maker can buy a stock for a lower price and theoretically sell it at a higher price is the market maker's reward for absorbing the risk of price fluctuation. For example, the quoted share price of

X CORP might be $16 bid, while the offer might very well be a quarter point higher at 16^1/4$. This means that an individual trader buying and selling at the quoted market would be able to sell stock at $16 a share but would be required to pay 16^1/4$ a share to purchase those very same shares. The quarter-point difference is the spread, representing the profit margin that market makers hope to secure. A day trader has to first overcome the spread before a profit can be made. Spreads are present in virtually every type of financial instrument traded—stocks, bonds, futures, options, etc. Dealing with and analyzing spreads is discussed in greater detail later in this book.

The second major disadvantage to the day trader has been the lack of access to the "real market." The securities industry has constantly tried to keep real-time quotes out of the hands of the general public. Even live business telecasts such as those on CNN and CNBC used to delay quotations by 15 minutes. And as of the writing of this book, Nasdaq still delays its quotations to the public by 15 minutes.

I have never understood why these delays are permitted to exist. Once a trade report is released, it becomes public news. The fact that the media still allow the news of a price to be delayed 15 minutes seems unconscionable; the media would not do it in the context of any other type of news. If one hopes to compete in the day trading arena, the knowledge of pricing cannot be delayed even for seconds. Unless an individual is willing to commit to an efficient quotation service, day trading is all but impossible. Most markets and exchanges display quote changes and pricing information *after* they occur rather than showing market movements while they are happening. Why this phenomenon is of the utmost importance and how it affects you are discussed later in this book.

COST OF COMMISSIONS

The high cost of trading—*commissions*—is another impediment to day trading success. Despite massive amounts of advertising claiming seemingly low commission rates for active traders—$10, $20, $25, $29 for any trade, any number of shares—you will find some of these advertisements are deceptive because they don't disclose the true price you pay. They don't tell you that the broker is getting paid off by the "contra" (other) side of your trade, a practice known as *payment for order flow*—usually costing you far more than the alleged discounted commission. The payoff *your* broker receives from the broker on the other side (the contra) in many cases equals or exceeds the commission charges your broker receives from you. Whom do you think your broker cares about more? You or the firm paying your broker perhaps millions of dollars annually? For example, you may be paying "only" a $14.95 commission on a trade of 1000 shares of stock, when in reality you very well might have been cheated out of an eighth or quarter point on the price. The effects of payment for order flow are discussed at length later in this book.

INSTANTANEOUS ORDER EXECUTION

Speed of execution of your order is another key factor. A successful day trader cannot tolerate any delay in the execution of his or her orders. Market makers (your real competitors) have immediate access to other market makers and can react in seconds to moving markets. A successful day trader must be able to do the same. As little as a 1-second delay can cause you to miss a trade—an almost insurmountable disadvantage.

Among the many advantages you will want in your trading execution system is your ability to execute your order virtually instantaneously by clicking your mouse button. Your system should automatically default to your preferred trading style by formatting your order instantly and extracting data from the quotation screen automatically to correctly price your order.

With the right computer system, the formulation and timing of execution of your order is in your own hands. The only delay in execution should be the time between the commencement of a market trend (or other decisional factor) and your reaction time in converting your idea into a mouse click that permits your trading system to format, enter, and execute your order.

Your trading system should also help you make a decision. An advanced trading system will have a market-monitoring function that will track any key indicators you deem pertinent, such as price, volatility, order size, and the like, and notify you instantly when a match is found. You can then make a trade, if you wish, by a few clicks of your mouse.

THE MARKET MAKER WINDOW

Chart 2-1 is a MARKET MAKER window. (Chart 1-1 contained two MARKET MAKER windows as part of the DAET computer screen.) The information in the MARKET MAKER window is broken into three boxes. The Nasdaq Level I information is the horizontal window at the top which displays basic information concerning High, Low, and Volume as well as the inside market of the highest bid and the lowest ask. The Level I box also shows the current price change from the pre-

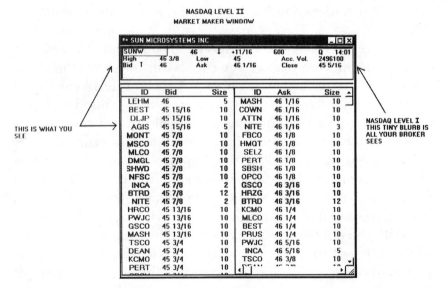

CHART 2-1.   The market maker window.

vious close. This is usually the only information made available to your broker.

The two vertical windows represent the "members-only quotes" and more importantly show order size (which affects the supply and demand) on both the bid and the ask side of the equation. The Level I and Level II data are constantly updated and refreshed by every relevant market transaction. Each participating market maker must display both a bid and an ask quote and can be executed against at its firm quote.

Size is quoted in multiples of 100 shares. The normal market is 10 by 10, meaning that the market maker is willing to buy or sell 1000 shares at its quoted prices.

Quotes on both the bid and ask side are listed by price, and all market makers willing to trade at the same price are color-coded, with the best price on the top of the so-called trading deck. As the price decreases, all market makers willing to trade at the lesser price are grouped in a different color, and so on down the price scale. When the market is volatile, the MARKET MAKER window scrolls up or down to indicate aggressive buying or selling. These price movements herald price change, which is the trader's opportunity.

You can have as many open MARKET MAKER windows as you can comprehend—and fit on your monitor.

INTERPRETING NASDAQ LEVEL II INFORMATION

As dealers adjust their quotations, the new prices are automatically displayed on the Nasdaq Level II screen. These changes are on line and therefore displayed instantaneously. The DAET trader closely monitors these second-to-second price movements and interacts with them by buying or selling these shares while the stocks are still moving—while the trend is still intact—rather than after they have stopped or even paused. This is essentially the DAET strategy. The "trend is your friend," and a skilled tape watcher can benefit from immediacy of execution by spotting the developing trend early.

One of the main attractions of your trading system should be access to multiple Level II Nasdaq quotes in a very user friendly format. The number of quotes and the quantity of other information you can see are limited only by the size of your computer screen. With the Pentium computers of today it is easy to set up multiple windows on your computer screen. Your trading system gives you the ability to have an order formatted and sent to the primary market by a click of a mouse and have your execution report back almost instantly.

The need for a conventional broker relationship is gone. In fact, *Time* magazine said it best when it ran an article entitled "Bypassing the Brokers." Brokers used to be regarded as professionals in the same hierarchy as doctors, lawyers, and accountants. Today, brokers are too often disdainfully treated like used-car salespeople, because they are often pushing stocks that the firm has underwritten or that the trading department is unloading for the firm's institutional clients.

I was amazed at how many experienced brokers working for major brokerage houses for years had never even seen a Nasdaq Level II screen. It seems like the real Nasdaq market is deliberately kept hidden from the typical broker. If the brokers are not allowed to see these quotations, how is it possible for the brokers to look out for their customers?

While other exchanges have order entry systems such as the DOT system on the NYSE, AMEX on the American Stock Exchange, and MAX on the Chicago Stock Exchange, these are order *routing* systems, which route or electronically direct the order to the appropriate specialist on the floor. While they work well, I have found that there are still too many idiosyncrasies and delays for my liking. The automatic execution of SOES affords a greater benefit to a trader. This, in conjunction with being able to possibly identify the emerging market trends in hundreds of Nasdaq stocks, is the mechanism of Direct Access Electronic Trading I currently prefer.

Actually, many DAET traders routinely deal in listed securities, and I look forward to leading the trend to fully automate the NYSE and become able to compete directly with the specialists. As far as I am concerned, specialists will soon become an extinct species.

REMOTE TRADING

Remote trading is now a reality offered by a few advanced DAET brokerage firms. Ease of execution is provided through a standard telephone line or an Internet connection. A class DAET firm will have a remote system that can operate over standard modems and deliver a high-quality remote service with all the features and benefits of a terminal located at the main office trading floor.

The typical DAET trader sits in front of a computer terminal displaying Level II quotations and all other relevant information. This service is usually provided by the DAET trader's broker-dealer at the offices of the brokerage firm; however, a superior trading system can now bring this service to the trader's home or office. The on-site DAET trader usually has an added advantage by being in a "fertile" brokerage environment where many ideas are exchanged, but those operating outside of the broker-dealer office have also enjoyed much success. Many traders feel they concentrate better in the quieter environment of their home or office as opposed to the noisier although more electrified environment of an active brokerage firm. I have a theory that remote trading may help one avoid being part of the "herd" mentality where you are likely to get caught up in the momentum of a panic move. Good traders capitalize on panic, and they are also seldom a victim of it themselves.

TRADING ON THE INTERNET

The Internet is a public network originally funded by the government to be an alternative communications network in case of nuclear destruction of the basic telecommunications network in the United States. Generally, the Internet is not sensitive to your interests. There are still several negative aspects of trading on the Internet. Unless you are using a business-based access provider, what you are saving in communications charges may cost you more in price execution, especially if you fall off the network or suffer a time delay in execution. Also, security on the Internet is questionable without proper firewalls and passwords. When you *need* access the most, the Internet will probably perform the worst. Public networks with millions of other users tend to render the worst service.

ON-LINE AND E-MAIL-TYPE TRADING

On-line trading through the Internet and other on-line services has burgeoned into perhaps the greatest growth area on Wall Street today. Trade execution and other services are being offered through the Internet by several on-line service companies. Eventually, trading on a secure business-based Internet may become the *generally accepted* method of electronic trading. The Internet is starting to be a great convenience to the investing public. The speed, dependability, accessibility, and overall quality of trading through the Internet has improved with the advent of broad-spine, business-based Internet access with enough bandwidth to afford real-time access to quotes and trade executions. Soon, you will never have to leave home except to attend an opera or a sporting event.

Internet access works for the geographically disadvantaged customers, who are far from cheap telephone service (such as those who aren't in the United States or are traveling). A first-class DAET brokerage firm has a vehicle suitable for Internet access with reserved access ports for each customer. Another major feature is real-time effectiveness of the quotation service being offered.

On-line services such as America Online and Prodigy say they offer stock trading services on the Internet. Don't be fooled. Your local access provider is the weak link in your orders. If you directly access your DAET firm, you want to be on a network instead of competing with kids in America playing Star Wars X-Wing with other kids in Japan. When your money is at stake, you need the most dependable access possible. You don't want to put yourself in John Glenn's position, who was quick to note that he wasn't comfortable riding in a space rocket containing thousands of moving parts each built by the lowest competitive bidder. You don't want to risk your economic life with a local access provider whose services are comparable to the defective rubber "O" rings which wrecked a multibillion dollar *Challenger* rocket.

Don't confuse DAET with ordinary e-mail-type electronic trading systems (like E-Trade, AmeriTrade, or E-Schwab). Investors think they are trading electronically when all they are doing is calling their discount broker on the computer instead of the telephone. The brokers love e-mail because they don't even have to pay anyone to answer the telephone or listen to the customer's complaints about the service or quality of execution.

When the market crashed in late October 1997, active traders with DAET trading machinery had no trouble executing their orders. Customers of Merrill Lynch and other e-mail-type systems could not even reach their broker because of the difficulty in logging on their trading networks. Many customers could not trade because their broker's system could not manage the market activity. In fact, your local telephone company generally figures that a small percentage of the population will be using the phone network at any given time. If everyone in the same city wanted to use the phone at the same time no one would get through.

There are positive aspects of the electronic trading revolution. The difference between the crash of 1987 and the crash of 1997 was the operation of the electronics and the circuit breakers. In 1987, brokers refused to answer their telephones in a meltdown market. In 1997, investors could execute their orders electronically as long as they could log on to their trading network.

Most people will tell you about the stock they wanted to buy at $10 but their broker told them that they were lucky to get the stock at $10^3/4$. Along these lines, I was showing my ATTAIN system to a large trading institution that was on the phone with its broker trying to buy 10,000 shares of a stock that I could see offered on an electronic communication network (ECN). The broker was reporting difficulty to the client and explaining how hard it was to find a 10,000-share block available for sale. The client saw the available stock on the Nasdaq Level II screen on my remote access computer and went wild. The result was one more customer for me and a kiss good-bye to the prior relationship.

For one who hopes to prosper as a trader, the quality of executions must be flawless. The executions must be fast and uncompromised, and reports must be instantaneous. Giving conventional brokers the opportunity to play with an order is an unacceptable position for a trader. Since the trader makes a living from the accumulation of small fractions of a point, there is no way for a successful trader to give up these fractions to a compromised broker or market-making system not operating in the trader's best interests.

DAET REPRESENTS THE FUTURE OF TRADING

To assure fair, fast, and accurate executions it is apparent that only an automated execution system will fill the bill. The Wall Street community has withheld automated execution systems from the public and continues to do so on major stock and commodities exchanges. The recent introduction of automatic quotation and execution systems is the technology that is paving the way for DAET to become an opportunity for the masses. For the first time in history, the individual can be as highly informed about market conditions as the market-making pro and have the opportunity to execute orders virtually instantaneously. The availability of instantaneous execution has severely eliminated execution risk, leaving only market risk as a deterrent to fabulous opportunity. As I stated earlier, with proper training and discipline, market risk can be readily controlled. *Conclusion:* DAET is one of the greatest opportunities to come along in this century.

Futurists tell us that 90 percent of the products we will be using 20 years from now haven't even been invented yet. For example, digital television, wireless communications, camcorders, PCs, and the like weren't around 20 years ago. Today, they appear in many households because they have been actively promoted and marketed by the industries that developed them. This analogy applies in reverse to DAET. Isn't it amazing that the leaders of this industry have not embraced this type of technology?

EXECUTION RISK

A first-class execution system used by the average person is the financial community's worst nightmare and your dream come true. The individual DAET trader does not have the fear of being abandoned, because there is always a way to get out of a position—simply by the press of a button. The trader may or may not be happy with the present market price, but at least Direct Access Electronic Trading gives the trader the ability to access that current price, whatever it may be. Your execution program does not tell you what decision to make; it merely enables you to take action and have your trade executed. Programmed trading already exists, but I believe that the individual trader wants to make his or her own informed decision based upon numerous criteria.

How many times have you told your broker when a market is collapsing, "Get me out at any price." The execution risk is an embarrassment to the market-making community because the quoted prices are not always attainable by the ordinary person. Option letters and trading strategies are published advising to buy calls and sell puts; buy four of these and sell two of those, and you have to make money. The advice sounds great in theory and looks great on paper, but many times it is impossible to execute. It would be easy for me to tell any kid how to pitch in the major leagues; throw strikes, work fast, and change speeds. The advice is easy to give but hard to execute. While execution risk is seldom discussed on Wall Street, I believe that DAET has to a very great extent diminished execution risk.

NO ONE TRADES WITHOUT A PERCEIVED EDGE

What makes Direct Access Electronic Trading a better opportunity than other types of trading? Why have people who have never traded before had such tremendous success trading through DAET? The answer is quite simple—Direct Access Electronic Trading levels the playing field for the individual trader. The elements present in Direct Access Electronic Trading are unique to the financial markets. While other day trading opportunities exist, to my knowledge only Direct Access Electronic Trading combines the use of the free flow of trading information and speedy execution. *The availability of trading information and the ability to act on it is the essence of successful day trading.* No matter what one trades, success will depend on identifying opportunities via analysis of available information (both technical and fundamental), making a conclusion (a trade decision), and then executing the trade.

Another benefit of Direct Access Electronic Trading is the virtually unlimited number and variety of stocks that can be monitored for movement and therefore for trading opportunity. For example, a person involved in day-trading a commodity such as gold or heating oil will be very disappointed or even bored if that particular commodity is not being actively traded at a particular time. Even if one is actually working on the floor of a commodity exchange itself, a dead day is a dead day.

Direct Access Electronic Trading, on the other hand, potentially involves monitoring hundreds of active Nasdaq and listed stocks. With rare exception, there is something going on somewhere in Nasdaq or the NYSE market. The Direct Access Electronic Trader goes to where the action is with the flick of a keystroke. It is unlikely that a commodities floor trader will run from pit to pit as easily as the DAET trader goes from stock to stock. There always seems to be a window of opportunity somewhere in the electronic environment. That's not to say one will always make money chasing this activity; however, an opportunity to profit almost always exists.

THE TICKER

Chart 2-2 illustrates a ticker displaying activity on the Nasdaq 100 index stocks. In order to qualify as a component of the Nasdaq 100 index a company must have a minimum market capitalization (market price times the number of shares outstanding) of $500 million and an average daily trading volume of at least 100,000 shares. Therefore, each of those stocks should be so well capitalized and actively traded that no one market maker could move the price.

You can customize your ticker to add (or delete) any stocks that you may want to monitor. Traders usually have a ticker displaying activity on the components of the Nasdaq 100 index and a ticker displaying activity on a selected basket of stocks.

TICKER DISPLAYING ACTIVITY ON THE
NASDAQ 100 STOCKS

Top 100 OTC Stocks		
NOBE [ISLD]	63 1/8	63 3/8
NOVL [ISLD]	10 13/16+	10 7/8
NOVL [INCA]	10 13/16	10 15/16
NOBE	63 1/8	63 3/8
COMS	1000	37 1/2
COMS	2700	37 7/16
COMS	200	37 1/2
BMET [INCA]	28 11/16	28 3/4
CSCO [INCA]	64 3/4	64 13/16
ADBE [BTRD]	0+	44 3/16
DIGI [MLCO]	18 3/16-	18 11/16
CSCO [MLCO]	64 3/4	65 1/4
CSCO	64 3/4	64 13/16
ADBE	43 13/16	44
NOBE [ISLD]	63 1/8	63 3/8
MCIC [MASH]	47 7/16	47 11/16-
KLAC [ISLD]	41 3/4	42+
COMS [DEAN]	37 3/8	37 1/2
ADBE [BTRD]	43 11/16+	44 3/16
DIGI	18 3/16-	18 5/16
KLAC	1000	41 7/8
COMS	1000	37 1/2
NOBE	63 1/8	63 3/8
ADBE	600	43 13/16
COMS	1000	37 1/2

CHART 2-2.   A ticker displaying activity on the Nasdaq 100 index stocks.

Tickers will scroll and dynamically refresh as any stock in the ticker is affected by market conditions. Note that the top stock on Chart 2-2 identifies the stock that is in play, the market-maker, price changes, and actual trades. The actual display is color-coded with green for a price increase and red for a price decrease.

DAET provides a way of operating in a very fertile environment where ideas become trades and trades become profits, and where losses can be quickly cut and profits can be allowed to run in the formative and idealized marketplace. The ability to access markets assures the trader that there is no need to delay the cutting of a loss—you can usually buy a stock back seconds later if you choose. Commissions are very low, and so the cost of active trading is not burdensome. The continued velocity and movement helps create a mind-set that prevents significant loss while providing potentially tremendous trading profitability. DAET traders make their money by grinding out profits and cutting losses quickly. If you want a big win, buy a lottery ticket.

THE REGULATORY FUTURE IS BRIGHT

The future of DAET is more radiant today than at anytime since I began my crusade in 1988. The reason is that since 1995 the Securities and Exchange Commission, under the enlightened and visionary leadership of Arthur Levitt, has become savvy to the inner workings of the markets. The successful introduction of new Order Handling Rules in January 1997 indicates that electronic execution in a transparent price environment is the order of the day. The names of the systems may change, but it is apparent that DAET is here to stay and will be the basis of the new market.

Direct Access Electronic Traders are not willing to pay tribute to the market makers for the simple act of honoring their markets, which the market makers are legally obligated to do anyway. DAET traders believe in the classic American position of millions for defense and not one cent for tribute.

The vast majority of Americans are basically antiprivilege and antielitism. While we believe in equality of opportunity for everyone, it is the availability of the opportunity that counts. The same thinking applies to the financial markets, where everyone desiring equal quote information and order execution should have the opportunity of unimpaired access. In fact, if we stand for anything as a country, it is the fall of undue privilege and the rise of opportunity. The business of America is business, and everyone should have an inalienable right to participate.

FIRM QUOTE RULE ORDER SIZE

For years I have stated that market making is a voluntary act. No one is forced into making a market. The minimum number of shares that market-making dealers are obliged to honor at their quoted price is now stated in hundreds (instead of thousands). This change was a direct result of the SEC Order Handling Rules and the development of ECNs. The firm quote rule was modified to coincide with the usual customer round lot order of 100 shares because the market makers were required to accept the customer limit order as their price (or send the customer order to the ECNs).

In January 1997, the SEC adopted an initial phase of a pilot program to test whether the reduced 100-share (down from 1000 shares) firm quote would reduce spreads and increase liquidity. At the time, the NASD's Small Order Execution System (SOES) constituency feared that the dealer's smaller firm quote obligation would put them out of business. The SEC agreed to test the lower firm quote on the top 50 (the "nifty 50") Nasdaq stocks. The nifty 50 was incrementally increased and is now up to 150. The NASD has filed rule proposals with the SEC to extend the "actual size" to all Nasdaq stocks.

Obviously, the market makers are dancing with glee. No issuer will have confidence in listing on the Nasdaq if the dealers are only willing to support the stock for 100 shares. I have heard that the New York Stock Exchange is saving the symbols "M" and "I" for Microsoft and Intel, respectively. So far, the management of both these issuers have been watching all-time highs in their stock prices and have no reason to flee the Nasdaq market.

Direct Access Electronic Trading is becoming more and more accepted and now constitutes a mainstream way of doing business. The old-line thinking was that electronic day traders were an aberration. Actually, DAET represents the future, and the current market-making environment is the true dinosaur. The market makers refuse to acknowledge that they are already being swept into the vortex of a dramatically accelerated evolution that will make the unadaptable extinct.

An electronic central market is obviously the way of the future unless you are deaf to the realities heralded by the new Order Handling Rules. A primary reality is the creation of many new trading facilities designed to accommodate public order flow and display public prices through ECNs. ECNs are being created to allow the public dissemination of limit orders which will interact with the current market-maker-dominated Nasdaq system. A customer limit order that is better than the market maker's quotation will be publicly displayed for all to see and thereby have a much higher probability of being executed than under the old procedures, when it would be hidden on the market maker's book. Market makers can no longer ignore public orders priced between the spread.

NEW ORDER HANDLING RULES HELP TRADERS

Day trading now includes trading on ECNs. I am talking about customer limit orders representing a better price than the national best bid or offer, which must be accepted by the market maker or delivered to the ECN for display. Accordingly, any order on an ECN could constitute a better price (or size) than the dealer quotes. Your trading system should hunt the ECNs and harvest these improved prices.

While this may sound simple, it represents the impetus for the changing market. Nasdaq is now converting to a customer-order-driven rather than the old dealer-quotation-driven market. Extensive investigations by the SEC and the Department of Justice found that market makers were all too willing to collude, conspire, and harass to keep the spreads artificially wide to the detriment of the public investor. The new ECNs make it far easier for public orders to interact in the real market and prevent the manipulative behavior of a restricted-access market run for the benefit of the market makers.

The concept of ECNs enhances price transparency by allowing public orders to be displayed. Price transparency means that the public has the ability to see the best prices from a variety of entities quoting a particular security. It also means that all secret markets should no longer be secret and all prices will converge in one place where the best prices will be prominently displayed, notwithstanding that Instinet still maintains a secret market. The creation of the ECNs is the first of a number of major changes that will evolve over the next few years. True depth of market with liquidity at all price levels will spring from instantaneous public participation afforded through electronics.

It is obvious to me that the future market will be a financial Internet where buyers and sellers of all securities will meet in cyberspace, obtain ultimate price discovery, and be able to have their trades executed instantaneously with no need for market-maker interaction.

BEATING THE SPREAD

It sounds quite simple, but transforming a good idea into reality (a trade) is often a very difficult task. For example, there are numerous books on trading option strategies—very often utilizing spreads. There are hundreds of "spread" ideas that are valid and theoretically possible. However, putting on the spread (actually executing all sides of the transaction) at the desired prices is a much more difficult task. Frequently, spreads cannot get executed within the theoretical parameters of the desired strategy. Floor brokers are usually charged with the task of setting up spreads, and your ability to fine-tune your situation on a minute-to-minute basis is virtually nonexistent. This can cause frustration levels to get very high.

Other problems are encountered in beating the spread: The quoted prices shown on the quotation services are not always accurate, specialists and market makers who are located on the trading floor "step" in front of your orders, and you as a customer are usually the last person to get serviced. Many times your "spreads" are executed only when no other "professional" wants them at that particular level. When I worked on the floor of a major futures exchange, it was common knowledge that "locals" came first—then brokers would worry about filling customer orders. (I recognize that I am mixing trading on an exchange with trading on Nasdaq in this section.)

MANY MARKET-MAKER ADVANTAGES HAVE BEEN ELIMINATED

Today, a quality trading system gives you all the information you need and executes your trade as quickly as possible. The major delay is the time that it takes you to make up your mind.

Simply put, the former market structure gave the industry professional so many advantages that the individual trader was most assuredly at a statistical disadvantage. This is similar to one's chances in a gambling casino, where virtually every bet you make is at a statistical advantage to the house. For example, in most casino games, even if you are an excellent player, the odds will be against you. This will ultimately spell disaster if you play long enough. Why do you think the hotel "comps" you if you guarantee to play for many hours? The casino knows the odds and relies on them to assure a relatively stable source of profitability based on overall handle. If you "card-count" and gain a slight statistical edge, the casino will throw you out. Wall Street operates in a very similar way when dealing with active day traders.

ADVANTAGES OF DAET

The advantages of DAET over other types of day trading include:

Immediate access to the market

Direct price competition

Low overhead operation

Guaranteed liquidity

Capability of spotting market trends

Capability of shifting to an active arena

Built-in discipline

Immediate Access/Assured Execution.   Day trading on most exchanges usually involves delays in execution of 30 seconds to several minutes. Even orders executed through "automated" systems such as DOT (NYSE) and AMEX (American Stock Exchange) are not automated order *execution* systems; they are actually *routing* systems, meaning that they quickly route your order to the specialist or market maker on the appropriate exchange for execution. Just because your order is quickly routed to the primary trading arena for that particular security is no guarantee that it will be executed at the quoted price you see on your quotation equipment. For any number of reasons, the trade you believe should be yours does not happen. Many times the quote is not accurate because of delays by reporters (exchange personnel who update quotes) in promptly adjusting markets (well, anyway, that's what you are told). Other times you are told that the stock "traded ahead," meaning someone beat you to the punch. In some markets, you don't get the trade you believe you're entitled to because of a "fast market." Simply put, when markets are active or in the process of moving, getting satisfactory trade reports from most exchanges is a nightmare. If you have had any experience in trading, I do not have to belabor the point. Getting imprecise execution and delayed reports has been standard practice.

Some exchanges claim to compete for order flow by executing certain-sized orders at the best quoted markets even if they are not quoting at that level. I have found that this representation is very seldom honored once the specialist on the competing exchange loses a couple of eighths. The offers to compete are only for "uninformed" order flow. If you appear to know what you are doing, the specialists want no part of your business.

Enter DAET and especially trading on Nasdaq—a system that essentially says "what you see is what you get," and you get it quickly, efficiently, fairly, and honestly. If the stock you see is quoted at a price and you are the first to access that price through DAET, it is yours—no stories, no excuses—just an executed trade and all within a few seconds. The system is impartial, legitimate, and efficient; it allows equal access for everyone and does not discriminate. It prevents market makers from "backing away" (failing to honor their market) and assures legitimate and liquid markets. The obvious result of this phenomenon is guaranteed liquidity for the DAET trader.

Direct Price Competition. Today, the DAET trader can instantaneously compete in the Nasdaq market at prices which can improve upon market-maker quotations. These improved prices have the effect of giving the DAET trader a greater advantage of getting an order at a better price and have a dramatic impact on narrowing spreads.

Essentially, placing orders through ECNs is turning a formerly dealer-driven market into a customer-order-driven market, which I believe offers a lot of advantages to the DAET trader.

Low-Overhead Operation. DAET traders can operate a business at a very low operational cost either from the offices of a DAET broker-dealer or from the comfort of their home or office, if they have affiliated themselves with a first-class DAET firm. At my firm, for instance, we do not charge rent, bill computer rental costs, or allocate utility expenses to the DAET trader. While remote traders provide their own PC, they may otherwise receive similar benefits. The cost to the trader is usually a small fee for the processing of the trade transaction.

Guaranteed Liquidity. The fact that orders (within SOES size/limitation) can be executed in seconds at the quoted market gives the DAET trader assurances of liquidity. Why is this so important? Primarily, because it enables the DAET trader to limit losses by being able to liquidate any unwanted positions in a matter of seconds regardless of how busy the market conditions are at the time the liquidation decision is made. As I discussed previously, and will emphasize continuously, cutting losses quickly is the key to trading success. In many other trading arenas it is not always possible to liquidate quickly, but in DAET trading it is routine. The peace of mind in knowing that you have hands-on control over your losses is the single greatest advantage of the DAET system.

Capability of Spotting Market Trends. Utilizing the Nasdaq Level II market quotations in conjunction with DAET execution allows the astute DAET trader, in many instances, to see previews of coming attractions, in that one can identify a trend in a stock early while there is still an opportunity to get in before the trend accelerates. By closely following market makers' price changes, an astute trader can many times observe a stock beginning to trend either up or down while still having time to access one of the remaining market makers before it has traded with someone else and has changed its price quotation. This enables the DAET trader to participate in the move while it is taking place. On other exchanges, the only basis for identifying a trend is by last sale price reporting, which tells you what *already* happened as opposed to what is in the process of happening. This is a subtle difference, but it can make the entire difference when day trading. Market makers, floor traders, and "locals" all have a similar advantage on the listed equity, option, and commodity exchanges. Now, for the first time, the DAET trader can also enjoy inside "flow" information.

In addition, a first-class DAET system will have an automated "tracker" program, which will monitor the entire Nasdaq market for any price movement you choose to see.

Capability of Shifting to an Active Arena.   Unlike day trading in one specific type of security, DAET traders can readily shift to any arena (stock) they wish to almost instantly. Someone trading gold, for example, often is quite inactive at times when gold is not moving around very much. Inactivity in the arena in which you trade does not present a profit opportunity. If there is no movement in the underlying security, it is virtually impossible to generate trading profits. Since thousands of Nasdaq and NYSE stocks trade every day, there are usually plenty of actively moving stocks that should meet the movement requirements of the DAET trader. For example, if Microsoft is trading in a narrow trading range, there might still be plenty of action in CISCO, Amgen, Intel, or any of hundreds of other actively traded Nasdaq or NYSE stocks. Each actively traded stock is an arena unto itself, and since there are hundreds to choose from, there is room for any number of DAET traders to be successful. No one need be crowded out. On many other exchanges, such as commodity futures exchanges, limited trading activity does not foster active participation by more than a few traders. If too many players enter the market, generating trading profits becomes almost impossible.

Built-in Discipline.   There is a limit to the number of shares a DAET trader can trade through the SOES system for any one order. At this writing that number in most cases is 1000 shares. The limited-size execution is for one transaction in the same security on the same side (buy or sell) during a 5-minute interval or sooner if you have become flat in the position. After 5 minutes or after turning over a position in a specific stock, the DAET trader is free to execute another trade in that security on the same side.

This limited number of shares tradable in one time period is large enough for most DAET traders to make a substantial trading profit, yet small enough to prevent a large loss if, in fact, the DAET trader maintains discipline. DAET traders can increase their activities during busy times to the extent of their capital by diversifying in several stocks rather than maintaining a high concentration in one or two. This diversification spreads ultimate risk yet allows unlimited upside potential. So while the rule restrictions may sound a little unfair, they are really advantageous in that they build in a discipline factor of limited size.

It is also possible for DAET traders to completely avoid the order-size limitations and the so-called 5-minute rule by trading solely on ECNs. Increasing order size, however, is not a form of lion training that I recommend for the initiate DAET trader. In the beginning and probably ever after, every trader should subscribe to the disciplines of trading.

IS DAET TRADING FOR YOU?

TAKE A SIMPLE TEST

You may have been itching to be a trader all your life. Perhaps you worked your way through college selling sweatshirts, bagels, or other items needed by your classmates. Or you may have been a baseball card collector or a shrewd buyer or seller. Many people just feel that they have the makeup to be one of the greatest traders in the world, just as many believe that they could have been a chess grand master. If trading interests you, take the following nonsocially scientific, fairly subjective test.

Do you desire a career change?

Do you want to be your own boss without the hassle of managing your own office?

Does corporate downsizing scare you?

Are you currently playing job-related Russian roulette?

Are you tired of commuting?

Have you hit a wall that will keep you from your earnings potential?

Does the idea of working from your home appeal to you?

Have you come to the realization that life is too short to waste?

Are you bored or unfulfilled—not yet ready to retire?

If you answered yes to several of the above questions, you may want to consider a career in the breathless and exciting world of Direct Access Electronic Trading. You may also want to consider the easygoing, pastoral life of a shepherd.

DAET AS AN OCCUPATION

DAET is unlike other businesses, which have a saturation point beyond which competition cannot exist. For example, there is a limit to the number of grocery stores that any neighborhood can accommodate. But I really do not see a limit to the number of people who can participate in DAET. DAET is growing every day and can accommodate continued growth far into the future. Don't let the future pass you by just because you fear competitive forces. Market competition actually betters the opportunity for talented traders.

The days when floor brokers would commute to the exchange, stand on their feet, and scream at other brokers for $6^1/_2$ hours are quickly vanishing. I can't understand why anyone would suffer the indignities of a trading floor and be a slave to the market. Trading is hard work. Many markets slow down for a while after the opening, allowing floor traders to take time to rest after the frenzy of trading the opening. With DAET, there should be no market dead time because the trader can comfortably and effortlessly trade in a civilized environment.

More people are becoming electronic day traders at a faster rate than ever before. Middle-management executives are getting squeezed out of their jobs in droves by corporate downsizing. Many baby boomers are becoming disgusted with the monotony and hassles presented by their careers, sometimes even those in the more respected professions such as doctors, dentists, lawyers, and engineers, to name a few. Many older people who are bored in retirement, younger people who are not finding the tremendous opportunities that existed in the past, and people who have loved trading their whole lives but never have had the means or the tools to participate on a minute-to-minute basis are all now participating in DAET. Older people with the time and resources to commit often find DAET stimulating and rewarding. People are turning to DAET trading for its prospective economic opportunity and the lifestyle it makes possible. It is ironic that the same computers that have put many people out of jobs are now affording the opportunity for a very stimulating and fulfilling existence.

Day trading can be an exhilarating and a pleasurable experience, and it permits tremendous personal freedom. You can trade for the number of hours you choose at any time that you choose (assuming that the market is open, of course). You decide where and how long you want to trade each day. You can take days off because you are not working in a conventional office environment with petty office politics and a boss overseeing your every action. There is no compulsory overtime or weekend duties. DAET traders can close out positions and "go home" at any time.

In essence, DAET is a wonderful occupation for anyone who is uncomfortable or unhappy in a standard corporate atmosphere and desires an uncomplicated working environment without interpersonal hassles. DAET is available to anyone with ability, skill, and sufficient capital regardless of race, gender, creed, sexual preference, or any other characteristics that are subject to bias or prejudice.

Also, there is no ceiling on potential trading profits. Some people want an unlimited opportunity because today's luxuries can become tomorrow's necessities, which is why no person has the biggest boat in the marina forever.

Today's Direct Access Electronic Traders can potentially make a decent living, in many cases surpassing earnings from their previous occupation. Trading success is the baseball equivalent of on-base percentages, not home runs. You don't want to be the Babe Ruth of DAET, where you strike out more than you get on base. Consistency is a meritorious goal. Small profits can quickly aggregate.

Your short-term trading goal should be to earn as much money as you need to support a reasonable lifestyle. Trading is a day-to-day adventure, which often results in financial gain and an enjoyable quality of life. You are investing in trading profitably and investing in a work environment in which you serve yourself as the ultimate boss and consummate employee.

In over three decades on Wall Street, I have never witnessed a trading technique that has the wide-ranging appeal of DAET. In the almost 10 years since I began training people in the successful SOES trading techniques, I have encountered many success stories. A percentage of would-be DAET traders failed, but only because they stopped following the DAET techniques and disciplines. The ones who followed the rules closely and did not hesitate have done exceptionally well. Some have become millionaires, and others are making many times what they ever dreamed possible. My system is self-cleansing, meaning that if you do not follow it you will probably lose money. If you do lose money, you may be required to deposit additional margin in your account in order to continue trading. At that point, you can stop trading altogether or you might want to alter your trading techniques.

PERSONAL QUALITIES NEEDED FOR DAET

Not everyone has a personality suited for DAET. DAET requires certain personality traits which, while not uncommon, are not found in everyone. The fact that you are interested enough to read this publication indicates that you possess several of the needed qualities. Many of the characteristics of the successful DAET trader are interrelated, as you will see as you read on.

Self-Confidence.   Trading is an art, not a science. In order to be a successful DAET trader, you must be confident with your computerized trading system and your training and you must follow directions and disciplines. There is no assurance that any particular trade will work out successfully, but you must always have a true inner confidence in the belief that it works out on balance and in the long run. This confidence keeps you going when you encounter a choppy day or are having a temporary losing streak. If you start to second-guess your trading ability and lose your confidence in the system, your chances of success are greatly diminished.

While confidence is necessary, when confidence becomes arrogance or stubbornness it can be fatal in the DAET arena. If your confidence evolves into stubbornness or arrogance, you will be very sorry, very fast. If you are too confident and do not quickly take your losses, you might very well get thrown out of the game—in other words, lose your capital. So while you need to be confident enough to make a decision quickly and act on it, you must also be confident enough to admit that you are wrong and reverse direction.

I have been electronically day-trading using DAET and its predecessors for almost a decade. It works—the results are well documented. If you are confident enough and work the system according to the rules, you, too, can succeed.

Focus.   Trading is a very serious business. Large sums of money are made and lost every trading minute. The ability to stay focused on the essential elements of DAET is vital for success. Constant focus on tape watching, order entry, and position monitoring should be uncompromising. Even a momentary loss of concentration can cost you hundreds or even thousands of dollars. The market continues to move whether you are watching or not. It does not stop because you go to lunch or take a coffee break. When you trade, you must be able to stay focused on your task and keep distractions to a minimum. For example, if you get distracted and lose merely an eighth of a point on 1000 shares of stock because you were late in getting in (or out), that represents a $125 loss. If it was a quarter of a point, that loss is $250. A distraction of as little as 5 seconds can sometimes cause these problems. Focus is a must.

Discipline.   Successful trading involves riding your winning transactions and immediately cutting your losses. Since winning transactions take care of themselves, the focus must always be on controlling the losses. That's where discipline comes in. If you are not disciplined, it will cost you lots of money. The problem is that people are very often reluctant to admit error and will not take a loss readily. A successful trader, especially a DAET trader, must be disciplined enough to take the necessary actions quickly and without emotional distress. If you can't do this—if you don't possess discipline—don't attempt DAET.

People who attempted DAET and failed did so because they did not possess the necessary discipline to cut losses short. They allowed trades to get away from them to the point where they lost so much money they couldn't continue trading. To succeed at DAET you must continue to play the game—you must continue to trade. If you are prevented from doing so because your capital is reduced too much, the game is over for you. You must have the discipline to cut losses quickly so the game never ends.

Good Memory.   DAET is twenty-first-century tape watching. Not only do you monitor your trading computer screen as the market makers change their quotes on Nasdaq Level II quotation equipment, but you also monitor DOT, check SelectNet and ECNs, try to identify trends, and quickly act on your observations. This requires a good memory for changing stock prices and the ability to quickly recall and analyze the various brokerage firms' quote changes. The better you can remember and conclude, the more quickly you will be able to identify a trend and act on that trend. Since there are hundreds of stocks that potentially can be monitored and dozens of different market makers quoting them, a good memory is certainly a characteristic a DAET trader would want to possess. The many new features of an enhanced trading system can significantly help your memory by providing alerts and sorting features that will assist your personal memory and enhance your vision.

Ambition, Hunger, Drive.   DAET traders on balance are driven to succeed. They can taste the financial rewards of successful trading. DAET traders certainly are not passive. They crave winning and abhor losing. They love the "action" DAET provides. The intensity of the game and the possibility of high financial rewards make DAET exhilarating for the people who can handle intensity and exhilaration. DAET is not a game; it is serious work with large sums of money routinely changing hands. To participate effectively you must be ambitious to the point where you are driven, whether you openly show it or are more controlled in appearance.

Competitive Attitude.   DAET traders are in head-to-head competition with market makers, institutions, and the general public as well as with other DAET traders. DAET is perhaps the most competitive arena outside of professional sports. And just as you do in professional sports, you know the results at the end of the game (trading day). All the traits described previously are needed in order to put you in a position to compete. However, having those other traits does not necessarily mean you have a competitive nature. The desire to win and succeed must be present if you wish to enter the DAET arena successfully.

DAET IS NOT INVESTING

DAET traders normally go home flat or close to it at the end of every trading day. On balance, Direct Access Electronic Traders do not hold a position overnight unless they have a very good reason to do so. It is normal for DAET traders to close out all positions prior to the close of business every day because they do not want to (1) tie up capital overnight and (2) subject inventory to overnight price fluctuations. At tomorrow's opening, the preopening situation and market-maker markups will tell you whether a stock is a buy or sell.

If you hold stocks for a longer term than intraday (especially overnight), then you have become an investor rather than a day trader. Investments involve a longer-term mentality and outlook than day trading, which by nomenclature is very short term. I tell people that if you want to be an investor, try real estate, mutual funds, and bonds. Or at the very least, come to understand that you voluntarily want to hold this position because you believe it will generate gains for you. There is a world of difference between holding an open position because you *want* to and holding an open position because the market forces you to postpone a loss that you do not want to recognize and pray will disappear tomorrow.

CAPITAL IS REQUIRED

DAET requires the availability of an adequate amount of capital. Your capital acts as your platform to extend your financial reach. Your capital is the tool that enhances your leverage.

Before the market was booming to new, record-setting highs every other day and stock prices were uniformly lower, you could have had success trading with $50,000 on margin. Today, probably $150,000 is the most advantageous amount of capital for trading, $100,000 is adequate, and $50,000 is a limiting minimum. These sums are based on the availability of margin under Regulation T of the Federal Reserve Board.

Remember that we are dealing with intraday margin. Intraday trading means price movements that occur from 9:30 a.m. to 4:00 p.m. New York time of the same day. Day traders usually trade the intraday volatility of securities and go home overnight with no exposed positions. And so no margin is usually needed overnight because the day trader rarely owns securities overnight.

Because Regulation T requires that 50 percent margin be posted as collateral toward the purchase price of most securities, your $100,000 of capital will allow you to buy $200,000 of securities at any given time. The current price or sell-short price of a high-cap Nasdaq stock may be over $135 a share, which translates into a purchase price of $135,000 on a basic 1000-share DAET order. Hence, your capital of $100,000 (when doubled by leverage to $200,000) gives you the financial heft to purchase 1000 shares of such a large-cap stock. As you can see, $50,000 of capital will stretch your available margin to $100,000, which will not be enough capital to afford the purchase.

Therefore, the amount of your capital limits your trading opportunities. This is why $150,000 of capital is more advantageous than $50,000. It is possible to run a DAET business with less capital. But you should understand that you must trade in the lower-price stocks, which historically may have lower volatility and may miss out on price movements in the highly capitalized, more highly priced, widely traded, and volatile stocks. Please note that many people start with $50,000 and build their capital base by shrewd trading.

Capital is a lot like a baseball bat. It allows you to get up to the plate and swing (trade). A larger bat may allow you to hit farther, but sometimes it makes it so hard to swing that your batting average can fall off sharply. Especially in the early stages of your trading, you should not commit an excess of capital to more positions than you can monitor carefully or your ability to close out transactions at the optimal time will be compromised. On the other hand, if your bat (trading capital) is too small, you will be ineffective, it will break, and you will strike out. Your bat—the amount of trading capital— should be sized properly for the type of hitter you are.

Most people feel that to be effective in the investment game you need a large amount of capital. This is very true—if you are investing. DAET traders *do not* invest; they trade. They buy or sell relatively small amounts of stock and turn their positions frequently. Therefore you only need enough capital to meet the margin requirements of the relatively small number of positions you hold at any given time. As a position is closed out, the margin required for that holding is available for another trade. This rolling in and out of positions allows a relatively small amount of margin capital to go a very long way.

Your trading capital will either grow or shrink from trade to trade depending on how successfully you have been trading. For example, if you make a quarter of a point on a 1000-share trade, your capital will increase by $250 less your commission charge. This increase is reflected immediately, and the additional capital is available immediately. However, likewise, if you experience a quarter-point loss, your capital will be reduced by $250 plus the commission charge.

At this writing, DAET utilizing SOES is normally restricted to trading a maximum of 1000 shares per trade. Even though the SOES maximum size limit is 1000 shares, you are still permitted to trade less than 1000 shares if you wish to do so. Since 1000 shares has proved to be the most optimally sized order, availability of margin capital should be based on a 1000-share SOES order trading size. Yes, you can trade more than 1000 shares at a time on ECNs.

Early in my DAET career I trained many DAET traders. Most started with a minimum capital base of $25,000 to $50,000.

THE LEARNING CURVE

A rocky beginning has become a more common occurrence over the past year or two. The added competition and sophistication of all players in general is creating a tougher environment for the novice. Training and simulated trading help keep the difficulties to a minimum for those students who heed the advice and lessons taught, but it is not unusual for the beginner to experience some losses at the outset. There is no teacher like a good old-fashioned experience, and no matter how hard I try to instill all the lessons of successful DAET, nothing ultimately works as well as a good loss in driving home the realities of disciplined trading.

Therefore, one should almost expect to have losses on the outset of trading. This is not a universal result but one unfortunately all too common. I call early losses "tuition" in that they are part of your training costs; and as long as the losses are small and tolerable, they should prove no problem in the long run for your DAET career.

Sometimes I think it's good for the new DAET trader to experience some losses early on rather than winning big right from the start. An early winner often gets a little too cocky and overconfident—this can spell disaster in the long run. A successful DAET trader is always a little scared of what the market can do and trades a little cautiously. Always maintain a healthy respect for the power of the market. No trader is bigger than the market. Just ask the Hunt brothers, with respect to the silver markets.

One of the self-cleansing effects of Direct Access Electronic Trading is that if, for some reason, you do not do well and your capital is reduced, you *must* replenish it or you cannot continue to trade. Margin requirements are a fail-safe mechanism. If you decide to stop, a good part of your capital should still be intact. Other types of endeavors frequently result in the entire loss of your risk capital. In Direct Access Electronic Trading your capital is always liquid and available to you (plus or minus your trading profit and loss). While you put your capital at risk, the risk is only as great as *you* make it. You assume market risk (trading risk), not capital investment risk or order execution risk.

OTHER INITIAL COSTS

Where can you go into business with virtually a limitless upside potential for a relatively small amount of money and with few administrative headaches? With Direct Access Electronic Trading you have unlimited earnings potential and yet you can go fishing or golfing whenever you want. The DAET workday is a scant 6 1/2 hours with no weekends or nights.

The cost of entering Direct Access Electronic Trading is relatively inconsequential compared with other potentially far less rewarding business opportunities. For example, the initial cost of entry into Direct Access Electronic Trading is much lower than the cost of a McDonald's or a Subway sandwich franchise, and you don't have to clean counters and sweep crumbs at the end of the day. One of the mottoes McDonald's tells its workers is that if there is time to lean (on the counters), there is time to clean. With DAET you can lean without cleaning. Furthermore, not only is DAET far from menial work, but it is also the ultimate in tradecraft and enterprise.

The entry costs are moderate. The initial cost involves your training, the acquisition of a computer, and a connection into an upscale DAET computer trading system possessing the special features you may favor. Your network should provide you with the proper access to the market. These start-up expenses do not cost more than a few thousand dollars. Your trading network system specifications may include a remote hook-up of your own IBM-compatible system so that you can always trade from your home or office if you so desire.

There are costs associated with learning how to trade. Proper training is the single most important factor for success. Your DAET brokerage firm should be able to provide the necessary education at reasonable costs.

FOUR

GETTING STARTED

INCREASED NEED FOR TRAINING

In the past years, the number of DAET traders has grown exponentially. A by-product of growth is additional competition among DAET traders as well as increased market-maker efficiency, which keeps the market makers' quotes in line and counters DAET order flow. As a result, new candidates entering the DAET arena must be well trained.

The fortuitous training of years gone by, when a student could simply look over the shoulder of an experienced electronic day trader, no longer provides sufficient skills to allow a new trader to successfully compete in today's environment. You have to truly understand markets and the psychology of trading.

Without proper training your chances for success at Direct Access Electronic Trading are greatly reduced. Even former market makers from major Wall Street firms have found how difficult DAET can be without the necessary training and background. DAET differs from the type of trading done by market makers, which historically make most of their money by working against customer orders. DAET traders, on the other hand, make their money by identifying trends, capitalizing on the spread, and acting quickly to participate in opportunities.

When Charles Darwin sailed on the voyage of the *HMS Beagle* in 1857 and published his *Origin of the Species*, he espoused the law of natural selection in which the smart, strong, and quick adapted to survive while the stupid, weak, and slow perished. Darwin theorized that survival of a species was based upon genetic advantages to the improved species due to mutation and adaptation to the environment over a long period of time. This biological theory of natural selection passed into the business climate of the United States in the late 1800s with the advent of the robber barons, who generally made an art form of lying, cheating, and prospering.

In theory, the age of the robber barons pretends to have ended largely as a result of governmental intervention designed to protect businesspeople from each other and to protect consumers and investors from the presumably predatory nature of businesspeople. But the concept of the survival of the fittest continues. Even today, we believe that the race is won by the fast, and in business we give credence to the cult of the astute. Friends flaunt patronizing the "biggest" doctor, the "smartest" lawyer, and the "best" stockbroker. No one boasts of having the most inept doctor, stupidest stockbroker, or dumbest lawyer. In truth, today humans don't have the time to adapt to the rapidly changing world by the process of mutation. We survive by creating our own environment, inventing tools, being mutually cooperative, and learning new skills. The competitive nature of business in today's global economy demonstrates that you must be trained for success if you have any desire to succeed before the market cleans your clock.

PAPER TRADING

Training begins with understanding bid/ask pricing, market-maker recognition, and reading the Nasdaq Level II tape. As you get more familiar with these data, you will quickly learn what the objectives are. At this point, getting comfortable with these fast-moving data is essential. The objectives are quite obvious—buy low, sell high or sell high, buy low. A new DAET trader observes developing trends, and in a relatively short period of time is usually ready to jump in and trade. *But not yet!* The neophyte should trade, but only "paper-trade," meaning that theoretical trades are made on a sheet of paper and graded to see how they would have worked out in real time in the market. The more seriously one paper-trades, the more one will benefit from the experience.

Paper trading should continue for at least two or three weeks and be conducted as if it were real. Some people need to spend more time paper trading, than others. You should allow for at least one week of supervised simulated trading. Accounting for profit and loss should be performed in the same way you would for real trades. Do not fool yourself. If you cannot paper-trade successfully, you are not ready to give up your daytime job or your money in order to become a trader. If you cannot shave balloons in barber school, you are not ready to use a razor on real people and spill real blood. A higher skill level and better results should come with practice and time. Paper trading, however, is a far cry from real trading because the emotions do not kick in. It is an excellent training vehicle, but not totally realistic because real money is not on the line.

THE START-UP ROOM

The next phase of your training should be a "start-up" room where inexperienced traders start trading with real money under the aegis of an experienced instructor. It is suggested that the callow trader be limited to a 200-share ticket (instead of 1000 shares) and receive a proportionately reduced transaction fee. We used to call our start-up room the "incubation room," the "halfway house," and the "hatchery," but whatever the name, the key was to stimulate the sixth sense by trading with live ammunition. This sixth sense is extrasensory confidence and situational awareness relating to the market. Newborn traders, however enthusiastic, should not self-destruct when they trade with real money. You should be allowed to remain in the start-up mode until you feel you are ready to trade—as long as you remember that a trader's education is never over. A trader learns something new every day.

The trader then opens a brokerage account, deposits the necessary margin capital, and is ready to proceed. At first the new trader will trade perhaps just one stock, either buying or selling short according to his or her sense of the prevailing trend. By watching just one stock, there is little distraction and the emotions of taking market risk can be felt. As the new trader becomes more comfortable with the machinery, his or her eye becomes trained to pick up the necessary changes. The trader begins to develop a sense of control. From this point on, the learning process accelerates exponentially. As electronic proficiency develops, the trader will grow to the extent that his or her talent and capital allows. If the trader doesn't achieve a minimum trading competence level in a few months, the result is the end of an opportunity and a way of life before it barely began.

THE REAL VALUE OF AN EDUCATION

It is hard to set a value on education. The cost of welding school is over $10,000. The cost of tractor trailer truck driving school is over $10,000. The cost of the education at a DAET program will vary but is less than the cost of learning to do welding or truck driving.

The purpose of an education is to prepare people for surviving in the real world. The tuition is inconsequential. Quality education is always well worth the cost. However, the money spent on a 4-year college degree could result in 4 years of beer drinking and partying. Even if this is not the case, after 4 years of college (and sometimes 5) you may wind up with no skills or trade. After a DAET program, you should have practical knowledge that will be of immediate benefit to you and your family. And if you decide not to make DAET your chosen career, what you learn about how the financial world works and how to deal in the market will still be of value since it will make you a better investor and expose you to the inner workings of Wall Street. Chances are that you will remember far more than you retained from the macroeconomics and accounting courses that you took in college. Basic theoretical knowledge is often forgotten the day the final examinations are over. Practical lessons about Wall Street are learned for a lifetime and reveal the otherwise mysterious world of financial trading as your perception of markets broadens your horizons.

You want to learn to think like a trader. You also want to learn how to learn. Your education as a trader and investor will never end; that's why the *Wall Street Journal* publishes a new edition every day. The news, business events, and their weighted interpretation are forever evolving. The objective of your training is to grow, mature, and change as an individual and to become a competent trader, and not just a DAET trader.

My strongest suggestion is to attend a quality training program. Alternatively, find a qualified DAET firm that has the expertise and is equipped to give the best hands-on training—it will make the entire difference.

CHOOSING A TRADING SYSTEM

The markets are changing so dramatically and the regulatory environment is changing so quickly that your trading system has to be a living system that is able to change as regulatory and competitive criteria dictate. What is state of the art today is old hat within months. In order to keep on the cutting edge of technology, your system will have to be updated regularly.

The only way for a first-class DAET order execution system to be faster than current standards is to insert probes directly into the human brain. Right now all that is necessary for an order to be executed on a premier trading system is to touch a button. Order execution is as fast as the click of a mouse. Until we can access the human brain or execute orders by telepathy, there will be no faster way to access the market and execute an order.

DAET furnishes market quotes, gives the essence of what you need to formulate a trading decision, and constitutes a user-friendly package to work an order to rapid execution. You receive exactly the information you need to enter into the financial jungle with snakeproof boots. No Direct Access Electronic Trading system can guarantee the profitability of your trades any more than any other tool can guarantee success. Just because you buy an Ernest Hemmingway Mount Blanc pen does not mean that you can write novels about the Spanish Civil War. It's how you move the chess pieces that win the game and not the quality of the chessboard.

Your trading system should access information and key you into the appropriate trading market. You should be able to customize your screen to suit your individual trading style and technique. You should not only have access to information but also be able to weigh the information to suit your trading criteria. Your trading system must help you to make intelligent decisions and grant you immediate access to the best price in the relevant core market.

The old-fashioned way of telephoning an order to a broker has gone the way of spats. When you telephone your order to your broker, you have no way of knowing when your order hits the trading desk or how promptly your order is executed. Direct Access Electronic Trading is a computerized system that permits self-directed executions of your orders via an appropriate broker-dealer trading system.

CHOOSING A DAET FIRM

So you think you meet all the requirements. You've explored other business opportunities and realize that DAET might possess the best potential of any of your alternatives. You have the personality, capital, and desire. You want to get started. You ask yourself: "How do I find a brokerage firm that can get me started? One that can properly train me, set me up with the necessary equipment, and provide me with the services I need to succeed?" Good questions.

Suffice it to say that finding an accommodating, teaching, and fertile DAET firm is probably the most difficult part of DAET. You should choose a firm that can spend the necessary time to teach you and set you up in an environment that will give you the highest probability of success, a firm that has a fertile environment where ideas flow freely.

When choosing a DAET firm, look for one that fits your personality and has patience with the new trader or inexperienced customer. DAET is very competitive. The firm you work through must be tolerant and untiring in its efforts to teach. Commission rates on a per-trade basis should be low, and there should be little tolerance for system failures. The pace is fast, and sometimes tempers may be short and intensity can run high. A good DAET firm understands this and takes novices under its wing and stays with them until they are capable of interacting properly with the more experienced DAET traders.

Remember—affiliating oneself with the proper DAET firm will be the single most important step you take in being a successful DAET trader.

There has been a proliferation of DAET brokerage firms. In fact, they seem to be opening up like fast-food franchises all over the country. On the surface, this appears to be good for the industry, because we must spread the word on the advantages of Direct Access Electronic Trading. The reality, however, is that some of the new brokerage firms view Direct Access Electronic Trading as a get-rich-quick scheme and are luring many people into the electronic trading environment without providing them with the necessary skills, training, and tools to compete effectively.

The easy-entry DAET firms have not invested the necessary capital in their programs or incurred the needed upgrade costs to constantly improve their trading systems. They have not committed the necessary time and effort to providing the extensive education required by new participants in order to increase each student's chances of success. In essence, a number of these new brokerage firms on the DAET scene have been lax in their procedures and short term in their outlook.

Many of these new entrants are already collapsing under the weight of their own inefficiencies and lack of technology. Their lack of capital and shoddy operations represent major problems waiting to happen. You want to think twice about trading at a firm that clears through a second-rate clearing firm. You want a reputable clearinghouse standing behind your DAET firm and holding your money. You will also want to see as much redundancy as possible built into the architecture of your firm's communications and trading network systems. You should expect your Direct Access Electronic Trading firm to demonstrate insightful management, backup at all the key management positions, and an internal technology department.

The management of your DAET firm should be of high integrity and run a business in compliance with all applicable rules and regulations.

CHAPTER

FIVE

PRELUDE TO TRADING

TRADING IS AN ART

Trading is an art. Just as there are many styles of art, all of which can be pleasing, there are many effective styles of trading—all of which can be profitable. While art appreciation is in the eye of the buyer, trading profits are much more readily determinable. I meet many people who are hoping that I will tell them the Wall Street "secret." They want to touch me and have me bless them with insight. Sometimes I feel like Obi-Wan Kenobi in *Star Wars* because people want me to tell them that the force is with them.

If you are reading this book to discover the Rosetta Stone translation leading to instant and eternal wealth, you can stop reading now. There is no magic wand that anyone can wave to make you successful, independently wealthy, and completely happy. There is no veiled incantation, magnetic lodestone, patented formula, or arcane process any one individual can use to move general market prices, because a market is millions of people interacting for their own personal reasons. By definition, every trade is a difference of opinion concerning the value of what is bought and sold. All I can do is give you my frame of reference, value structure, trading tips, and lifelong observations of what works and what doesn't.

I am willing to tell you what I know, but only you can make it work. Computers, bricks, pavement, concrete, real property, and seats on stock exchanges do not of themselves make money for people. Only the ingenuity of the human mind can turn capital resources into income-producing assets. Likewise, only the creativity of the individual can parlay stock price movements into trading gains.

The insight of the guru is tantamount to the power of the wicked witch's ruby red shoes in *The Wizard of Oz*. Those ruby pumps could harness lightning bolts for the witch but turned to anchors on Dorothy's feet. Just as the true power of the magic shoes was always within Dorothy, successful trading may lie within you. I am going to share my insight and experience. Trading is risky, and your ability to handle risk in a businesslike fashion will increase your chances for success.

TRADING IN GENERAL

People trade goods and services virtually every day of their lives. Most people call their trading a "job," where they trade their services (talents and skills) for monetary compensation. Others barter directly for goods or services. The ability to trade astutely can make the difference between increasing or decreasing value received.

Most people who have a passion for trading visualize themselves in a major Wall Street trading room buying and selling millions of shares of stock, similar to scenes they see at the beginning of *Wall Street Week* on PBS. The thrill of wheeling and dealing with large sums of money and stock is a fantasy that many market participants would love to have come true. The runaway bull market of the last 16 years has convinced perhaps millions of people that trading in the financial markets can be incredibly lucrative and more entertaining than Siegfried and Roy. In reality, this can be true. However, the rewards of trading are not automatic, and much training, work, and discipline are required. In addition, financial capacity must be present, along with the ultimate realization that one can fail in this endeavor.

RISK

Direct Access Electronic Trading does not guarantee profitability. What it does guarantee is that you will be able to interact in the market in an efficient and timely fashion. If you choose to buy, you can do so immediately; if you want to sell, you can do so immediately. DAET allows you to turn your ideas into actions (consummated trades) and your actions into profits (or losses). DAET allows you to maximize your pricing in between the spread. You have the ability to advertise a better price to the entire marketplace—thereby allowing you the opportunity to make a little more or lose a little less. Remember, in day trading fractions count—*they count a lot!*

The concept of risk is familiar to all of us. Basically, the question of risk involves how far you are willing to lean over the edge of the carousel in order to grab the brass ring. Risk and reward depend upon the circumstances. A trader is one who will take a calculated chance on one less fact than anyone else. The decisive quality separating the true trader from the remainder of the populace is the willingness to take calculated risks. For this reason an understanding of risks and risk taking is important for the potential trader. The amount of risk you are willing to take depends upon the situation, other options, and the amount of capital you can afford to lose.

Two basic risks exist in DAET. The first risk is a market risk. If the market price moves in the opposite direction of where you want it to go, you could lose money on the trade. The second risk is an execution risk. This is the risk of the inability to execute the trade at the desired price, or at all. The execution risk is seldom discussed in the investment community because your broker doesn't want you to know that his or her firm may not be willing or able to execute your trade at what you deem to be an appropriate price.

MARKET RISK

Market risk is normally controllable if you employ proper discipline and diligence. We all accept reasonable market risk every time we buy any product. Everyone who trades takes a market risk because stocks go up and down. That is the nature of the market and that *is the nature of the opportunity.* Strategies exist to handle market risk. Perhaps, most importantly, you need a personality that can tolerate market risk in order to trade successfully. The wherewithal to deal with risk varies from person to person. If you are averse to taking a market risk, then put all your money in certificates of deposit in Federal Deposit Insurance Corporation–insured banks or in short-term U.S. Treasury bills, assuming that you trust our government for 91 days at a time.

Let me emphasize that market risk represents the opportunity to make profits. Market risk is universally and indivisibly related to any investment. All actions in life involve some risk; you could accidentally choke on a Big Mac or one thin french fried potato.

EXECUTION RISK

Execution risk is the problem of turning an idea into a consumated trade. Just because a stock appears to be quoted at a certain price does not always mean you will be able to buy it at that price. Historically, execution risk had reduced the odds of success. The Nasdaq market was structured to maximize the opportunity for brokers and dealers. Fees, commissions, spreads, and trading "costs" were the price each customer paid to use the market. Those costs were built into the system. Each customer took on a little sliver of the added costs so that no single customer felt the pinch enough to complain. Execution risk can diminish profit like friction drains motion. Eventually, even the slight friction of the tires on the road will stop any vehicle.

There is probably no doubt at all in customers' minds that execution is faulty. Even worse, one of the greatest fears of investors and traders is being shut out of the market, where they would be hanging in limbo, helpless to take any action to alter their situation. This fear has a real and fairly recent basis. During the crash of 1987 investors and traders could not reach their brokers and react to the falling market. Even if you got through to your broker, your broker couldn't get through to the trading desk; and even if your broker reached the trading desk, the trading desk was unable to contact the floor brokers, or in the case of Nasdaq, the market makers. The result was a complete breakdown in liquidity and in confidence in the existing market mechanism.

Customers fared somewhat better during the crash of 1997. In 1997 electronic systems and electronic interfaces made the market makers available even if they didn't answer the phones. Even so, many electronic systems melted from the overload. Large brokerage firms such as Merrill Lynch refunded damages to customers.

People also have a real concern about the slippage that frequently occurs in the execution of their orders. As I stated on national television, I do not believe there is a person in this country who has interacted with the brokerage community in the execution of a trade who has not felt screwed. I have had dozens of customers who have come into my office tell me horror stories of how they have been skewered by their brokers, including full-service brokers, discount brokers, and even deep discount brokers. And my travels and discussions with industry professionals indicate that not only do individuals feel cheated but so do institutional investors, who know that they have been treated poorly by the market makers and the system.

Angry customers complain about prices that seemed inconceivable based upon quotes received when entering their orders. They feel frustrated because they feel they can do nothing about it. The remedies offered by the industry are impractical in that the expense, time, and effort to protest in an arbitration proceeding make such an exercise seem futile. Therefore the only way to assure a fair execution is to place yourself in a position of getting the correct information immediately and have the execution performed immediately with full knowledge of the current market. Putting faith in your broker to do the right thing is like Little Red Riding Hood trusting the wolf.

Public investors and traders were willing to accept any number of market-related mistakes and errors but were not willing to accept institutionalized disadvantages programmed into the order execution mechanism. The systemic shaving of fractions of dollars on trades still costs the investing public hundreds of millions and perhaps billions of dollars annually. When the house in any casino routinely takes a cut of each transaction, the losers don't care because they have no financial interest in the transaction and the winners don't complain because they won. In the market, however, the investor was positioned to absorb the dollar slippage on the buy and the sell side of the transaction every time, because the industry believed that the investor had no where else to go. The investor had to pay the tribute. Eventually I was no longer able to stomach the system and decided that the true American way was to pay for defense and not for tribute. Defense took the form of DAET. And I have found that when people have an informed choice, they will almost always opt for DAET as a viable alternative.

TRADING INFORMATION

The objective of the trader is to assimilate information and then logically make transactions that will result in realizing profits in the course of execution. Since it is illegal to obtain inside information—information that is not available to the public but that will have a direct impact on the price of a stock—a trader must gain information in more indirect ways. Research recommendations, rumors, technical analysis, and the like are the meat on which the trader feeds. The astute DAET trader uses responses to his or her orders as a primary indicator of where short-time trends are going. Although there are dozens of systems that chart and analyze market movements, these systems are of little use to the second-to-second and minute-to-minute trading techniques employed by DAET traders. I have found that the most important information comes from the actual trades I am involved in. For example, suppose I hear about a weakness in regard to the price action on a particular stock; however, if I am bidding for those shares and no one hits my bid, then it is clear to me that the reported weakness may be hype. Alternatively, if I am offering stock at the inside price or better and no one sees fit to lift my offer, a report that the stock looks strong may also be market hype. A trade in a security means that money is changing hands and that has always proved to me to be the real deal. Talk is cheap, but a trade is a trade. While people are more than willing to give you their insight (which all too often can be self-serving), putting their money on the line is usually a more reliable indicator.

Knowing this, the active trader can strategically place orders in a system and gain real insight as these orders are executed against. For example, if I were offering 1000 shares of Apple at $18^7/16$ and a while later my machine reports that it was automatically sold, I would immediately look to see if the stock was ripe for an upward move and seriously consider buying even more shares at $18^1/2$, figuring that the upward direction was confirmed by the fact that my offer was taken. I am realistic enough to know that I know nothing about intraday pricing on stocks; therefore, it is reasonable to assume that the person buying the stock from me may be more informed about the near-term outlook concerning the stock. If in fact the stock is about to make a move up, I will be fortunate enough to reap the rewards of the upward move; and if I am wrong, I hope I will have the discipline to cut my loss immediately and move to another trading opportunity. The important thing to remember is that the directional indicator was not a graph or a chart, but rather an indicator that was generated by a real trade, one that was personalized for me and therefore known only to me. With the significant reduction in trading spreads today, this technique can be very effective and relatively inexpensive when misinterpreted. This technique is the most popular method I use when trading. I call this "Putting Your Money Where Their Money Is and Not Just Where Their Mouth Is." An actual trade is the real deal.

This concept is elaborated upon by closely monitoring the actual execution of transactions on your trading system's SelectNet screen, ATTAIN, Island, Instinet, TNTO, or other ECN tickers. On these systems, you can observe actual pending orders being executed against. Observing bids and offers being taken is the next best thing to being involved in the transaction. Naturally, in order to see these transactions taking place, you must have a system displaying this information.

Some people believe that a time and sales ticker will provide the same kind of information described above; however, a time and sales ticker does not indicate which side of the transaction initiated the trade. Was the bid hit or was the offer taken? A competent trader who is able to understand the screens will have a distinct advantage over those who follow general technical analysis procedures, especially when trading on a very short term basis.

TREAT TRADING AS A BUSINESS

The business of Direct Access Electronic Trading has become a serious business rather than a casual pursuit of quick profits. DAET is a business where the entry costs are relatively low, there is no inventory to carry, and there is no need for sales contacts. If you are trading on a trading floor (in one of my branch offices, for example), you don't have to pay for electricity, telephones, fax machines, copy machines, or even a computer. Thus, there are few barriers to entry.

As discussed above, you will need access to capital (which is your money) in order to meet the regulatory intraday margin trading requirements. The amount of capital you will need can be controlled somewhat by you and your trading pattern. If you trade heavily in high-cap, high-price stocks, you will need more intraday margin. At the close of the market, you should leave flat so that your capital is held in the form of cash and not subject to overnight fluctuations.

For a few thousand dollars in training expenses, you can be in business with all the education, training, and equipment you will need. Where can you get into business today for less than the cost of a high-end automobile and have the potential to make huge profits? This is not pie in the sky. I have successfully trained people who were formerly gardeners, hairdressers, and even lawyers. Some of the people who have done well had only 15 cents in their pocket and a willingness to compromise when they first arrived in this country.

The DAET traders who are having the most success have expanded their horizons by treating trading as a serious business venture. Managing a business includes devoting time and being dedicated to the affairs of the operation, hiring assistants, keeping proper books and records, maintaining trading strategies, subscribing to publications that give ideas and tips, attending conventions, and, for remote traders, buying state-of-the-art computer upgrades. Making trading a business also means having a strong focus and paying careful attention to detail. I have generally found that if you take care of all the small items, the big substantial matters either take care of themselves or have already been anticipated.

Assume that you opened a franchise business. It could be any kind—a Subway franchise, McDonald's, a Blimpie, or even a bagel store. The first thing you would do is hire an assistant. You wouldn't even think of working store hours—18 hours a day and weekends. Your assistant would do the chores you didn't want to do and cover in your absence. Your assistant would more than take in enough in additional revenues and profits to pay the weekly wages. The same goes for DAET.

It is extremely helpful to have an assistant who monitors loss control or scans for market movement in order to help you seek profitable situations. It is very easy to hire and train an assistant to provide a second set of eyes and reflexes. Any subordinate you hire should more than pick up an extra quarter of a point each week of profit or loss control, which will more than pay for the person's salary expense. College help is available at $7 an hour times 35 hours a week. This equates to merely one quarter of a point a week. If your assistant cannot save you a quarter of point a week, you have hired the wrong assistant.

Computer literacy is to your assistant what the slide rule was to me. A helper gives you extra eyes to watch the screen. An assistant takes the pressure off you. You tell your assistant that you don't want to take more than an eighth of a point loss on this trade. Loss control now becomes the helper's job. The helper does not have any emotion about the stop loss, whereas you (perish the thought) may abort your own orders and decide to hold the stock for an additional loss out of a false sense of pride. An assistant will help you maintain discipline on the loss side of the equation.

Your assistant will help you find value in the market and also help prevent loss. Your helper can scan *Investor's Business Daily* for stocks on your daily watch list such as yesterday's most active, new highs, new lows, and whatever else excites your trading appetite.

Also, the availability of an assistant means that you don't have to close your office when you're out. Why shouldn't you be making money while you are playing golf?

However, don't confuse the ability to have a good lifestyle in business with the business of business. Sure, you can take an afternoon off. You can take a long lunch. And you can take a day off from time to time—but not every day! You are your own boss in DAET. You have to make sure that you act responsibly as your own boss and, in fact, become the toughest boss you ever had. In the business of trading, time, capital, and skill are your inventory. You need to spend the time to grasp opportunity when it comes your way. You never know when that tidal wave of price movement will wash in your direction. The 3-point increase or drop could occur at the opening as well as the closing of the market. You want to be there when it happens.

Managing your own business means that you will undertake a minimum amount of paperwork. By and large, your trading system and your broker's clearinghouse should prepare the paperwork for you. You will want to review the computer runs for accuracy so that the "Flying Dutchman" of cyberspace doesn't roost as a trade on your statement. Your computerized trading program should also generate a daily profit and loss statement.

STRATEGIC ALLIANCES

People who love the concept of DAET but don't always have the time or the head for trading can now participate in this tremendous opportunity through the use of *strategic alliances*.

A strategic alliance is a partnership between an investor with capital but no desire to trade and a trader with ability but no capital. This is a classic marriage of money and brains.

Talented traders are more difficult to find than people with surplus capital. People with capital can search for a decent trader and enter into an agreement in which the trader and the investor can share the trading profits. The investor provides margin capital for the trader, who is willing to work all day for a hefty percentage of the profits a gifted trader can generate.

Perhaps the most readily available form of strategic alliance can be found at the firm where you want to train and trade. For those traders possessing a smaller amount of capital than is required for trading on one's own, but available as risk capital, a very palatable solution may be possible.

A basic concern of a day trader is the amount of leverage available to conduct intraday trading activities. Naturally, the greater the leverage, the more open positions the trader can carry at any given time. Leverage is a double-edged sword because it cuts both ways. It has been my experience that there are many potentially excellent traders who have limited access to risk capital. To facilitate their capital needs and nurture this trading talent, a new strategic alliance opportunity is being offered by some firms, including mine, to extend the increased leverage offered to broker-dealers to qualified traders, allowing those traders to trade with the firm's capital. Naturally, there are certain requirements, restrictions, and risks that go along with this opportunity, but in many instances such an alliance may furnish opportunity to candidates with limited capital resources.

SUCCESSFUL TRADES COUNT

A competent day trader really does not care what type of instrument he or she trades. To the day trader, all the various securities are merely an assortment of letters written on a trade ticket or a computer screen. It makes almost no difference what you trade as long as you trade it successfully. For example, a half-point profit on 1000 shares of General Motors stock has the same profitability ($500 gross) as a half-point profit on 1000 shares of Apple Computer, a half-point profit on 100m IBM bonds, a half-point profit on 10 option contracts, a half-dollar profit on 10 gold futures contracts, a half-point profit on one U.S. Treasury bond futures contract, etc.

The bottom line is that the mathematics of trading securities works the same no matter what you are trading. You don't care if you are trading horse manure futures or Treasury bond futures: A profit is a profit regardless of what you trade.

Market price fluctuation is one of the keys fueling intraday trading. One form of happiness for DAET traders is active, dynamic, and rapidly moving stock prices. In the old days, a nonvolatile market used to be a problem for the Direct Access Electronic Trader. Today, even in the dullest of market days, there is always some stock on the run which is a proper trading vehicle. DAET includes exchange-listed securities as well as Nasdaq securities. The number of moving stocks is too much for the human eye to behold, so top-quality trading systems have an automatic analysis program watching all the stocks and streaming the movements you want to review to a special ticker on your computer screen. Even with the most refined search parameters, there should be action on your analysis program.

Even in a nonvolatile market, there will always be stocks that are good candidates for the market-maker style of trading. The DAET should be able to set a range within the inside market which can result in profitable trades through buying on the bid side and selling on the ask side.

STYLES OF TRADING

The reason that your trading has a chance to prosper is because you are unique. You are the only person in the world who is you and possesses all of your special talents, gifts, ideas, and insight. You will have your own ideas about how to trade and like any gifted student will soon surpass the master. In order to deal with your creative process, you will have to take measured risks.

What trading technique (style) will you employ? Although from the outside most DAET traders look the same, subtle differences exist in every trader's style. Basically, all you do is identify a trend, enter, wait for the anticipated move to occur, and then close out accordingly. Seems simple and basic, but within this "simple" scenario are many possible variations, variations that can make major differences in your profitability. There are several techniques you can employ; all will work with varying degrees of success. The most important thing is to be consistent with whatever style you choose, rather than continually changing.

MARKET-MAKER-STYLE TRADERS

The earlier methods of trading focused on momentum trading techniques. Since the implementation of the SEC Order Handling Rules in January 1997 and the proliferation of ECNs and access to them through DAET, new techniques are available which can be employed to enable profitable trading. Most of these techniques will allow the successful trader to prosper by applying market-maker techniques that were formerly the exclusive domain of the brokerage industry.

Simply stated, the results of the SEC's Order Handling Rules and the implementation of the ECNs have made it simple and efficient for traders to initiate *quotes* and/or *trades*. Previously, brokerage firms had no obligation to reflect your limit orders (quotes) in the national market mechanism. In addition, your broker could take several minutes to execute your order against a quoted price.

Today, initiating quotes and trade executions is virtually instantaneous. Limit orders that improve the inside price must be displayed to the entire world. Initiated quotes are now nationally disseminated, and the completion of customer trades against firm quotations has come down to a mere mouse click. Since the act of trading involves initiating trades by hitting quoted bids and taking quoted offers, all strategies must operate within this framework. The logic behind trading can be varied, but the implementation of a trade must be done before one can expect to make (or lose) money.

For all practicable purposes, the Order Handling Rules have created the opportunity for the average person to compete directly with the market-making pros. Through ECNs, any trading entity (individual, institution, money manager, hedge fund, investment club, etc.) can place limit orders that will be reflected on the Nasdaq screen, thereby giving that entity the same competitive advantages the market-making community has enjoyed for decades.

This new trading situation must be driving the market makers crazy, because the DAET traders are now creating their own wiggles and jiggles. The fact is that this new opportunity exists and will be expanded upon until a truly level playing field exists in all the financial markets. In addition, the SEC rules have dramatically reduced spreads, thus giving all trading entities the opportunity to quote in smaller increments. No longer do market makers have to compete only with each other; they are now forced to compete with every limit order. This fact will surely make it more difficult for them to post the record earnings they have been showing for many years.

A market-making style of trading involves using the spread to your advantage rather than having to overcome it. A market-making-style trader looks for stocks that are very often not as volatile as momentum trading stocks. The securities that a market-maker-style trader usually trades have a modest spread and do not fluctuate significantly in price. The objective is to buy on the bid side of the market and sell on the offer side, making the spread the significant portion of the potential profit, as market makers have done for years.

Spread cutting, where a trader competes on price rather than favoritism or payment for order flow or general good old boy techniques, is a strategy that has suddenly appeared. Despite the fact than many spreads have already been reduced significantly, there are still countless opportunities for a market-making-style trader to compete on a price-competitive basis since there are almost 6000 Nasdaq stocks. As soon as ECNs can compete head-to-head with exchanges, thousands of more stocks will be available for price-competitive trading.

Since market-making-style traders utilizing ECNs do not have the ability to pay for order flow, it stands to reason that only better pricing will entice the other side of the trade to come to them. As spreads tighten, market makers will be less ready to pay for order flow because they will be forced to compete with the superior prices being posted by ECN participants. The hope is that this phenomenon will make paying for order flow uneconomic and create an atmosphere for a truly competitive marketplace where orders will automatically route to the best prices, regardless of who is posting them. The only criterion should be the validity of the quote and the assurance of a consummated transaction.

Market-making-style traders will also utilize this competitive bid and offer technique in conjunction with the "putting your money where their money is and not just where their mouth is" scenario. It works because while the market-making technique means that the other side of the trade comes to you, you will still be able to initiate the execution of trades electronically through DAET. Therefore, if you are willing to stay liquid and cut your losses quickly, you can control your positions through DAET and not wait for someone else to initiate against your bids and offers all the time.

GRINDING

Many traders, the ones I believe do best, employ a low-tolerance, high-velocity (LTHV) trading style. This means they get in and out of their positions very quickly and have a very low tolerance for loss. These traders watch many actively traded stocks, get in fast on seeing a trend developing, grab a quick eighth or quarter point, and say good-bye. If they cannot get an eighth, a sixteenth will suffice. If even that does not come and the trend appears to be reversing, they will sell out flat or even at a small loss almost immediately. They realize one thing: Stocks do not "wear out"; you can trade them over and over again and they remain the same. If the LTHV trader gets out too soon, she or he can reenter once again; the "trend must remain their friend." This style requires constant focus and attention. It is called *grinding* because the trader is continuously grinding out profits eighth by eighth and quarter by quarter. This technique generates many transactions, and total commission costs are higher than with other techniques; however, in my experience the grinders have had the greatest overall success with the least amount of real exposure. The LTHV trader seldom reads business newspapers such as the *Wall Street Journal* or *Investor's Business Daily* or listens to financial news reports. The LTHV trader's sole reason for making a trade is price movement. The trader does not care why a stock is moving, only that it is moving. The trader does not analyze stocks or care about fundamentals—only short-term price movements. The LTHV trader goes with the flow and maintains no opinions. This may seem easy, but if one possesses the other traits necessary for DAET, it may be very difficult to "have no opinion." Finally, the grinder virtually never takes home an overnight position.

SPECIALISTS

These DAET traders "specialize" in a handful of very actively traded stocks and concentrate only on as few as 5 to 10 stocks. The stocks they will trade, such as Microsoft, Apple, CISCO, and Intel, are the most active of the active stocks. Specialists develop a feel for these securities and utilize DAET, SelectNet, and ECNs to enter and exit them freely. Since these securities almost always have significant intraday moves, there is plenty of opportunity to catch swings. In many cases specialists work in teams so they never miss even a small blip. This intense concentration on relatively few stocks gives them confidence that a situation will never get away from them because of an oversight. Specialists make extraordinarily good money by sometimes "pressing" their positions, that is, increasing them to more than one lot (1000) as the trend continues in their favor, within the restrictions of SOES regulations. Risk is minimal for specialists because they have a handle on all their positions at all times. The novice DAET trader is best advised to start as a specialist before venturing into the grinding arena. Those who do not have the head—the extensive memory—for grinding are also best advised to play the DAET game as a specialist. My clients acting as specialists have generated handsome profits. The specialists usually know a little more than other-style DAET traders about the stocks they trade but not so much as to develop a strong opinion. The most important information to know is when earnings are to be announced and other relevant information that might cause a price movement at a particular time. Fundamental analysis is not very important and should almost always be avoided.

PARAMETER TRADERS

The parameter traders are similar to the grinders except that instead of jumping in and out of a stock very quickly, they allow for larger interim moves (both for them and against them) but within a disciplined parameter. For example, if they buy a stock and it does not go up immediately or declines slightly, they may stick with it for a while, but within a predetermined parameter (perhaps a half point). If the stock continues down to where the loss is a half point, it is then immediately liquidated. On the other hand, if it goes up, they will usually hold a little longer to maximize profitability. It is not sold out for the first eighth or quarter profit, but rather held for the potentially larger profit. The benefit of this technique is that you do not get chewed up by a choppy market. Your tolerance for a little more "pain" can help avoid the continuous buying and selling that a stagnant, choppy market can create. This technique can also save a little in commission charges, but if the parameters are not strictly heeded, large losses will occur. Only the most disciplined Direct Access Electronic Trader should employ a parameter strategy. It is useful for the DAET trader who is a little more laid back in his or her approach and cannot readily handle a grinder or specialist approach.

SHARPSHOOTERS

Sharpshooters methodically watch the tape and screen, entering only when they are "absolutely" sure a good trading opportunity exists. Unfortunately, being absolutely sure is far from absolute. Because stocks usually look best at the top and worst at the bottom, sharpshooting is very difficult. Direct Access Electronic Traders sometimes become sharpshooters when they are in a slump, thinking that by trading more slowly and deliberately they will do better. The fact is that they usually don't. DAET traders usually try getting into a "rhythm" with the market and flowing with it. The "trend is your friend" is the attitude most DAET traders live by. Being methodical and cautious are good traits. But if being overly so takes you out of the flow if—those traits keep you from "pulling the trigger" and participating in the trend—then they could be causing more harm than good.

Since nobody knows which trend will be real and extended, the DAET trader will often get jiggled in and out of a stock. This is part of the game, and there is no way to prevent the small losses created by jiggles. They are irritating as hell, but an integral part of DAET. Without jiggles and some losses, everyone would make money on every trade; therefore everyone would be a DAET trader and therefore there would be no game at all. Thank goodness for modest losses!

FADING THE MARKET

As the market is becoming more and more volatile and more players are playing the direct access electronic game, sophisticated traders are starting to trade more like market makers by fading a move. Fading is the practice of selling into strength and buying into weakness—going contra to the trend, because of the many intraday direction changes that occur. As more and more trend traders come onto the scent, the opportunity for traders will be even greater. Once again, if you fade the market and turn out to be wrong, you must immediately cut your loss, just as you would in any other strategy.

DIVERSION TRADERS

A diversion trader is someone who loves the action of trading but has another full-time profession or is perhaps retired. Businesspeople, doctors, lawyers, engineers, etc., are often bored with the routine of their professions. They use DAET as a diversion from their regular career activities. Since DAET is very short term in its nature, anyone can participate for even a short period during the day. The excitement and intensity invigorates these DAET traders, and usually they find it a wonderful escape from their everyday world. All they need is a Level II quotation service and a remote hookup into their trading system and they are all set to participate in this exciting arena. Usually these Direct Access Electronic Traders stay in the most volatile, actively traded stocks so they can participate in the action and get the moves they seek in short periods of time during the day. Their styles vary, and DAET is done as much for the enjoyment of trading as it is for gain.

OCCASIONAL WINDFALLS

The nature of the DAET business is such that on average about once a month, or at least every couple of months, there is an unusually large, intraday move in an active Nasdaq stock. An active Nasdaq stock is one that is very often traded by the majority of Direct Access Electronic Traders (e.g., Apple, Microsoft, Intel, CISCO). On occasion an active stock will be the subject of takeover speculation or other news and move several points in a matter of minutes. The astute trader utilizing almost any style will jump in on these situations and usual make a windfall profit. Although instances like this do not occur on a daily or weekly basis, they do occur on average about 6 to 10 times a year and are a real shot in the arm to DAET. While most career Direct Access Electronic Traders do not count on these windfalls, they do occur fairly often and are very instrumental in significantly increasing the annual income of the DAET trader.

As we approach the central trading market, these windfall dislocations should fade away. Most significant corporate news is now announced after the close or before the opening, in order to minimize the intraday price impact on the stock. The result is that traders are less subject to the major intraday swings that can generate a windfall profit or loss. As long as traders go home flat at night, they are not subject to major market moves. For better or for worse, the days of major windfall gains and exaggerated losses have been dramatically reduced. I think this is a good consequence—it diminishes intraday tension and so there is less worry about trading being halted in a stock you are holding.

HYBRID STYLES

After reading and analyzing all the different trading styles that can be employed, it is most likely that a qualified candidate will develop into a "hybrid"—one who will assimilate various aspects of the different styles in the attempt to become uniquely individual and a profitable trader. No one method of trading works all the time in all market conditions. It is important that whatever styles you use, you use them with consistency and adhere to basic discipline. You can use market-making techniques or momentum techniques (or other techniques) so long as you don't use different techniques as an excuse to trade with wild abandon. The trading techniques are tools to be used to help you trade with your brain and *not* with your gut instincts when loss tolerance is involved.

Every person brings special talents to trading and must deal with special weaknesses. Trading discipline is designed to put limits on your trading style and attempt to assure that you do not blow yourself out of the game before you become proficient.

Hybrid styles work exceptionally well in certain circumstances and not in others. For example, a grinder and a market-maker style of trading are very compatible, while a market-making style does not necessarily integrate well with a sharpshooter style of trading. Again, remember, the several styles are not to be used as excuses to trade too loosey-goosey.

FERTILE TRADING ENVIRONMENT

A fertile trading environment is the most important factor in making sure one participates and rarely misses exceptional price moves that could be exploited. In a fertile environment, many DAET traders work in close proximity with one another and many eyes are monitoring stocks. If a stock "breaks out," it is usually spotted by someone who passes along the information, thereby allowing everyone who wants to participate to do so. DAET traders working on their own at a remote location might miss this action because they might not be monitoring that particular stock. As they say on Wall Street, "A good idea can be worth a lot of money." A quality trading system will have a mechanism for displaying all in-house trades so that if a great deal of activity occurs in a particular security, the remote customer has the ability to pick up on the action.

HOW TO TRADE

THE KEY TO SUCCESSFUL TRADING IS DISCIPLINE

Most of the best traders I know are consistently successful because they hate to lose money and are motivated by fear. They respect the market like a sailor respects the ocean. Good traders know that they must contain a loss immediately and then focus on making money on other trades. The discipline is to move "paper" continuously and not fall in love with positions. Good traders don't look back; they only move forward. Trading to them is as natural as breathing and as automatic as walking.

The formula for success is making correct decisions, which includes taking profits and containing large losses.

WHAT GOES ON IN THE MIND OF A SUCCESSFUL TRADER

Why does one person spot a trend before another? Why can two people look at the same computer screen and come up with different perceptions about what is happening? There are skills to trading that can be learned and instincts that are inborn but can be honed. A trader has to be able to observe its prey like a cat, sit and wait patiently, and then pounce at exactly the right moment with a decisive action. Jump too soon and the prey runs away. Jump too late and the opportunity is over.

Successful traders turn their positions. Among the indicating events they look for are:

1. A pattern of updates of quotes by market makers

2. Price movement in stocks related to other stocks that have already moved in a similar industry or group, such as the high-tech industry where secondary stocks may follow the price movement of a major stock

3. Inactivity in a stock for a relatively long period of time (this time period could vary from minutes to days depending on the stock) and then one or more market makers changing their quote for no apparent reason (not necessarily going to the best price)

4. News and earnings

5. Early identification and participation in trends

6. General trading momentum on various exchanges

7. Unusual activity that does not look right with respect to a stock

8. Events talked about by business commentators who have the ability to affect the market, such as the commentators on CNBC, CNNFN, and/or the major networks

9. Brokerage firms' upgrades and downgrades of stocks

10. Knowledge of when a company will report earnings and the market effect of actuals compared with expectations. A company's reported earnings compared with the earnings expectations by the major brokerage firms that follow that company and its industry

11. Trading activity on various ECNs

12. Significant moves in bond markets, commodities markets, precious metals

13. Statements from the Federal Reserve, unemployment statistics, PPI, CPI, and the like

WIGGLES AND JIGGLES

When I first started to utilize SOES for trading back in 1988, it was relatively easy to spot trends, enter quickly, and exit profitably. A handful of traders represented the entire SOES trading community, and competition between SOES traders was virtually nil. The only opposition was the leading market-making firms; unfortunately they comprised the major committees of the NASD, which passed numerous rules and regulations restricting SOES trading. Since 1988 I have been the primary advocate fighting for the individual rights of the DAET trader.

Today, the NASD and its regulatory attitudes have changed and are easier to live with than they were. Changes in the rules have encouraged many more people to trade electronically. It is generally more competitive to DAET/SOES-trade now than it was in 1988 due, in large part, to the increased number of participants vying for the same stocks.

Having more DAET participants has led to the phenomenon of significantly more "wiggles and jiggles and head fakes." For example, when several DAET traders decide to buy Intel at the same time, several market makers might move up their quotations as they each sell a small quantity of shares. Other market makers will copy the actions of the first market makers and move their price quotation, without even making a print (trade at their quoted level). Market makers have begun to realize that when DAET traders come in to buy shares, it is only a matter of time (usually only a very short period) until they will be offering to sell back those very same shares. Knowing this, several of the more astute market makers will start to "fade the trend" (sell into the DAET buyers) and then downtick the stock, causing DAET traders to maintain discipline and sell out. This type of action creates what I call "wiggles and jiggles." Stocks go up (or down) a small amount, stop, and reverse—sometimes several times a day. This type of action can drive DAET traders nuts.

There are defensive measures DAET traders can use to counter wiggles and jiggles. The proliferation of many DAET traders into the arena has the effect of sucking up liquidity almost instantly. If three market makers are on the inside ask price and twelve electronic traders try to buy at the same price, the price level can quickly be absorbed. The antidote is for the DAET trader to be more anticipatory in trading style rather than waiting for "just one more" price movement to confirm momentum.

Since it is almost impossible to know for sure whether a perceived move is the beginning of a significant trend or just a jiggle, the DAET traders must act on their best judgment and hope for the best. If you get jiggled out, so be it. Persistency and discipline must always be maintained. There will be days when you get wiggled and jiggled like crazy, but that is a reality and a cost of doing business. On balance this reality, if handled with good business sense, can be kept under control and does not deter the successful DAET trader. The overall advantages of DAET trading significantly outweigh the difficulties created by the wiggles and jiggles.

HEAD FAKES

Head fakes are a problem similar to wiggles and jiggles. Whereas wiggles and jiggles are created by routine market-maker actions that have come about through their increasing experience in dealing with DAET traders, head fakes seem to be more deliberate. Head fakes are movements by a market maker or market makers (sometimes in concert) designed to create an illusion to induce market participants and the DAET trading community to take an action (i.e., buy or sell). For example, if a market maker wants to create selling (the market maker is really a buyer), the market maker would have a few market-making "friends" initiate a downtick at about the same time. This gives an illusion of weakness, and there is a good chance several DAET traders would be induced to sell shares into this staged decline.

After the selling is completed, these conspiring market makers would quickly reverse the trend and "catch" the

DAET traders. Often head faking occurs around lunchtime. SOES traders used to joke that lunch hour head fakes appeared to be a game created to amuse market makers. On reflection, the head fakes were probably caused by the internalization of orders during the lunch break while the market was slow. Furthermore, after the NASD consent agreement precluding collusion, I wouldn't readily expect collusive head faking. The NASD and the market makers have already been chastised by the SEC for fixing prices and have agreed in a civil action to reimburse in excess of $1 billion in civil damages (in my opinion far too little).

Head fakes can be costly, but once again, just as in the wiggles and jiggles scenario, they are part of the business and overall do not have to be a significant negative in your DAET career. Licking wounds will not change anything because all of the trader's time and emotion is being focused on a losing position and many profit opportunities are being squandered.

DEFENSIVE STRATEGIES AGAINST WIGGLES, JIGGLES, AND HEAD FAKES

To lessen the affects of wiggles, jiggles, and head fakes, most DAET traders try to trade only stocks that are very active with a relatively large float and capitalization. *Active large-cap stocks,* as they are known, such as Intel, Microsoft, CISCO, 3COM, etc., are much more difficult to wiggle and jiggle. They trade so actively and there is so much institutional interest that it is very difficult for a market maker to move them around or create any false illusions.

Perhaps the best way of dealing with wiggles, jiggles, and head fakes is to take advantage of the ECN trading where any trading entity can now interact with the inside pricing of Nasdaq stocks by placing competitive quotes and sizes that are displayed as part of the inside market. This practice impedes the market makers' ability to move stock prices without committing significant capital. In order to move a price the market makers have to fill all limit orders displayed on Nasdaq before trading at an inferior price. "Trading though" is a violation of current NASD regulations and is reportedly a regulation that will be enforced.

In addition, the instantaneous nature in which new competitive quotations from any trading entity can be placed into an ECN for display on Nasdaq makes it more difficult for a market maker to artificially move the price of a stock because a new quote with additional size can pop up virtually at any time, defeating the strategy employed by that market maker.

ECNs can help or hurt any trading entity trying to orchestrate a market move. The ECNs have made true market depth an unknown factor in that new orders can be placed immediately, preventing market makers' ability to gap stocks short term. Previously, market makers used to move prices in the moments it took to display additional size or improved prices.

These factors with the soon-to-be-adopted decimal pricing will further decrease spreads and make wiggles, jiggles, and head fakes potentially far more costly and uncertain to those trying to create them. Head fakes will be reduced because the SEC and NASD are watching and take a dim view of collusion. Also, telephone calls in trading departments are being monitored on a continuing basis. Firms will have a greater interest in not exposing themselves to penalties because of the greed of any single trader.

Since the publishing of my last book, market makers have finally accepted the reality that Direct Access Electronic Trading exists now and is here to stay. This realization has already caused all market makers to change their trading style and techniques. A trader should not agonize when turning over positions actively. If DAET traders stay liquid and nimble, they will put themselves in the path of profit. Some people become suspicious when I advise them to trade actively, aggressively, and often. Suspicious people feel that because I own a brokerage firm, it is in my best interest to advise people to trade often. While it is true that the trading fees I charge customers fuel my business, it is also true that my most active traders are also those traders reaping the most profits. Fluid trading styles propel the trader to take trading profits quickly and, more importantly, not hesitate in taking losses at the appropriate time. Fluid traders enter and exit the market aggressively and never agonize over a particular trade. To them positions are just computer bytes representing opportunity to make money.

By trading actively and often, one automatically learns not to agonize over taking a small loss on any single trade. This trained willingness to move out of a losing position routinely puts the trader in a position in which he or she will never incur a loss of more than a few hundred dollars on any one position. This keeps the trader's head "clear." The biggest problem of letting losses go beyond a very small fraction of a point is not only the actual dollar loss on that position but rather the fact that the trader stops being productive because he or she is focusing on losing instead of making money.

DEPTH OF MARKET

Instantaneous access leads to far greater depth of markets. Depth of market means the amount of stock that can be traded at a given price. For example, if a stock is bid at $21^1/8$, how many shares can be sold at that price before the price would have to trade at the next lower price?

A great deal of rhetoric had been flowing concerning the depth of market on various exchanges. Competing exchanges espouse the theory that their respective markets are tighter and offer greater depth than other exchanges. For example, a representative of the NYSE recently spoke about depth of market on his exchange, explaining that since spreads have dropped to one-sixteenth, the depth of market at each trading interval had decreased but overall depth of market had increased based upon total price. It all sounded profound, but actually there would be far greater depth of market, in my opinion, if the NYSE allowed all trading entities to display quotes and sizes instantly as they can now on Nasdaq through ECNs. I believe that size on the NYSE would be much larger if it weren't for the well-earned mistrust of specialists which all too often leads large buyers and sellers to withhold order size because they believe the specialist may try to trade against the order to the customer's detriment.

If a mechanism existed for instantaneous access to the inside market with instantaneous dissemination of the improved price and size, orders could be placed by "upstairs" (off-floor) market participants anonymously and immediately, thereby providing far superior depth at all price levels. The specialists fear this scenario, as well they should.

DAET allows any trading entity to interpose its limit order and size on Nasdaq instantaneously. No longer are prices dependent upon market makers' quotes because any trading entity can enter its own quote and size at any time.

FINDING THE "AX"

Spotting market trends and quickly acting on them is at the heart of DAET profitability. But how does one really know or at least have the highest probability of identifying a "real" trend as opposed to just another market jiggle? This is often the toughest question of all. Who exercises power and who runs away? Your ability to answer these questions will ultimately determine how successful you become in your DAET career.

All market makers are not created equal. The DAET trader soon learns to respect powerful market makers and pay attention to their actions. I do not believe there are more than a dozen market-making firms in this category. While many firms are the Ax in a stock from time to time, very few have significant influence on major DAET stocks (stocks often traded by DAET traders) on a continuous basis. Major SOES stocks are usually the better-capitalized, actively traded, higher-priced Nasdaq stocks (Microsoft, Intel, Apple, CISCO, etc.). The "real" market makers usually trade all these stocks and seem to have orders in hand or an inclination to heavily position these shares at all times. You can assume that they will not run for the hills when a few small orders come their way.

Perhaps the best or at least the most often used factor in analyzing a move is to check out who is behind the move, meaning which market makers are moving their quotations. Certain market makers seem to be more of a factor in certain stocks than others. The market makers that seem to be the biggest factors are usually the firms with the largest institutional clientele. Firms like Goldman Sachs, Salomon, Lehman, Bear Stearns, Morgan Stanley, and Merrill Lynch handle a great deal of large institutional order flow and are more likely to be "real" in a stock. Being real is a way of describing the probability that they will usually stay at a quoted price and trade rather than run away from their quoted market. These dealers many times have large orders in the stocks they trade, which make their markets real, or they at times will commit a good deal of "firm" capital to a position when trading a stock.

In contrast, most market-making firms very rarely desire to hold positions or commit firm capital and only look to get a piece of the action on the orders they can work against (known as "getting in between orders"). These firms get their orders in exchange for payment for order flow or soft-dollar arrangements to institutional and retail firms and then flip the shares for small fractional profits. Firms such as Mayer & Schweitzer, Herzog, Troster, and NITE are well-known trading houses that usually trade size only when they have an order in hand. They seldom commit capital to position trading and are usually not real factors in pricing (without an order in hand). They trade for the spread.

In all too many cases, a market maker is in a particular stock only in the hope of "catching an order," an order it can trade against. What I mean by "trade against" is that the market maker will quote a price for a stock based only on the premise that it can turn around and fill an order it already has in hand—risklessly. If the market maker has a buy order, it can buy stock against that order knowing it can always sell that stock to its buyer—risklessly. Alternatively, if the market maker has a sell order, it can offer stock "short" knowing it can buy the stock back from the seller, also risklessly. It's a "no-brainer" and almost always profitable. These market makers have no desire to position stocks (keep an inventory) and are only a factor in a particular stock when they have an order. Their influence is temporary, and they very seldom quote the inside market. The fact is that most market makers are not very interested in taking risk.

Naturally, almost any market maker can be a significant player in any particular stock at any specific time; however, the powerful market makers named above seem to exert influence on an ongoing basis. Knowing where they are at all times is a good policy to follow.

Certain market makers, though few in number, are the movers and shakers in the Nasdaq market. These firms usually handle many institutional orders and commit significant capital to the positioning of various stocks. There are many times called the "Ax" in the stock. If not the Ax, they are at least "real" market makers. With today's enhanced transparency and the proliferation of ECNs, market makers, including the Ax, are very capable of disguising their orders. For example, the Ax in a stock may very well show itself to be offering shares at the inside offer when in fact it is bidding for shares through another market maker (stooge) or anonymously utilizing the services of one of the several ECNs.

Therefore, you must always keep in the back of your mind that the picture you see may not really reflect the intention of the Ax. These people are not stupid and certainly do not wish to draw you a road map of where they intend to go. The Ax is a firm that has a particularly large interest in a specific stock. Sometimes, that interest may have been as an underwriter or selling group participant in the shares, research coverage, ownership interest, or a big retail position in the stock. Sometimes, there is more than one Ax in a stock.

If one observes a stock for a period of time or reviews the company's filings on the SEC's EDGAR database (incidentally the Internet website for EDGAR is http://www.sec.gov/), the identity of the Ax will become obvious. Initially, the Ax may be identified by observing who very often "stops" price momentum in a stock. "Stopping momentum" in a stock means remaining at the offered price when the stock is moving up and conversely staying on the bid when the stock price appears to be dropping rapidly. The substantiality of a market maker's bid or offer is dependent on how much stock the market maker is willing to buy or sell. In general, it should be noted that an Ax may become irrelevant at times when the stock's momentum and volume are high because usually no single market maker is bigger than the market. Once the Ax in a stock has been identified, you may use this knowledge as *one* of the factors in making a trading decision.

In my earlier book I included a then very valuable chapter that rated market makers' significance relative to their impact on the price of the stocks they traded and identified those market makers that were just along for the ride. While there are still several significant firms that make meaningful markets in a multiplicity of stocks, it is much more difficult now to evaluate their impact because there are many ways to disguise one's influence in a stock. Orders can be placed through ECNs, and decoy market makers may be acting on behalf of the more significant players. In addition market makers of substance have merged or in other ways evolved into new entities that are harder to analyze. It is no secret that firms like Goldman Sachs, Morgan Stanley, Bear Stearns, Salomon, and Smith Barney are still names to be reckoned with. I find it more difficult, however, to really place the significance I once had on the impact of even these firms.

The Department of Justice and the SEC investigations have heightened the awareness of market makers concerning collusive behavior on the part of renegade traders. Therefore, any single firm's dominance without the involvement of friends seems unlikely. This will diminish the influence of any single market maker. Due to the new reality, I believe that detailed market-maker ratings could in fact be more misleading than helpful.

"TRADING-THROUGH" VIOLATIONS

The NASD formerly had a reputation of seldom enforcing "trading-through" violations (a practice that some say continues even today). Trading through occurs when a transaction takes place at a price that is inferior to the best quoted market on Nasdaq. For example, if the inside market on Apple Computer is $18^1/2$ bid and $18^5/8$ offer and a trade is reported at a price of $18^3/8$, it is apparent that the seller of the stock was cheated out of an eighth of a point because the seller was entitled to at least $18^1/2$ (the quoted bid) on some quantity. The brokerage firm that executed the order in fact traded through the best bid ($18^1/2$) and thereby denied the seller the superior price. This is a despicable practice that violates a firm's fiduciary obligation to its customer and NASD regulations.

Despite this fact, this practice occurs *all* too often. In order to ensure fairness, it is every trader's and investor's obligation to report these types of improprieties and protest them with vigor. Only then will firms respect the sanctity of the central market system, thereby assuring the fairness and integrity of the equities markets. Remember, ignoring these seemingly minor petty offenses only makes the violators bolder and almost legitimizes their actions.

For years the brokerage industry knew full well that most investors would not have the initiative, time, or money to object to "trading through" and other reprehensible behavior. Only an informed public can keep the brokerage community honest.

If you see stocks trading through your limit, call your broker and insist on a report of the particulars. If no remedial action is taken, file a complaint with the NASD. If you are still not satisfied, then contact the SEC, which is basically your last bastion of sanity before you go to court.

THE ART OF TRADING

Trading is an art that can mature into a skill. It is not a science. If trading were a science, I could teach you all the rules, regulations, techniques, and stratagems and everyone would be a successful trader. Everyone would be rich, no one would want to work, and you would have to grow your own food and do your own laundry. In other words, if everyone were rich, no one would be rich. There would, in fact, be no advantage to being rich.

If art were a science, everyone could be given paint and a canvas and would paint the *Mona Lisa*. Imagine a world long on *Mona Lisas*. The price would drop to nothing. Every museum and family would have its own *Mona Lisa*. *Mona Lisas* would be found at every garage sale.

You can have red paint, blue paint, and yellow paint but you may not create a work of art, just as a trader with a computer is not yet an accomplished DAET trader. To become an artist you have to learn perspective, color, and shading. To become a trader you must learn to interpret facts like price changes to turn them into potential profit. Even with the technical knowledge, you may not become a master painter; but with the proper training you should be able to create a picture that is identifiable and somewhat pleasing. A trader who is well schooled and disciplined should be able to make a living. A millionaire? Maybe, maybe not. A good living? Yes. Just like art.

The value of your trading artistry is defined in dollars and cents. You could give a thousand people a thousand computers with the same information screen, and some people will see a breakout to the upside and others will see a topping action. One will see a stock drop as a crash, while another will see the same move as a major buying opportunity. The ability to make the proper decision and the results that follow will determine who has painted the real *Mona Lisa* and who is just finger painting. We all could have access to the same facts, but we weigh the decisional factors differently. The strength of your training program will determine how well you learn your basics in decision making regarding the evaluation of facts.

BASE YOUR TRADES UPON FACTS

In science, a fact is something that you can verify with your five senses. You can see, feel, hear, taste, or smell a fact. A fact is independently verifiable. Unfortunately, facts are usually only a fraction of the iceberg. Collecting facts does not always lead inexorably to the proper conclusion mainly because you can never be sure that you know all the facts. Suppose a company looks outstanding on a fundamental and technical basis. Unbeknown to you, a large holder of the shares may be having serious financial problems due to an event that has nothing to do with that particular security. The large holder is forced to sell his large holdings over a short period of time, causing a major downward move. You are right about the company but wrong about short-term direction.

We make decisions based upon facts. However, most of us have trouble distinguishing facts. We also have difficulty in the degree of reliance we can place on any single fact. Moreover, there is such a torrent of information that we cannot recognize which facts are more important than other facts. Before you make a trading decision, you will want to verify the facts as closely as you can. You will also want to assess the source of the facts. Most of the time, the statements of fact that we rely on come from sources that we have not independently verified. When the weatherman states that it is now raining, I can look for myself in order to verify the facts. But when the weatherman predicts tomorrow's weather I can't verify that forecast. And rather than rely on my own assessment, I may tend to believe that a professional prediction of a proposed fact is better than my own.

Assessing and evaluating the source of "facts" is crucial. The view of the facts espoused by the chief executive officer of a company may be especially biased. Remember that facts can be sculpted, twisted, bent, and restated. Lawyers manipulate facts all the time. There are lies, damn lies, and statistics. When it comes to statistics, "figures lie and liars figure." So carefully examine the facts upon which you base your trading decisions.

Also the facts may change. Sometimes our perception of the facts was incorrect or the timing of the facts was incorrect. For example, it may stop raining. When you see that the facts have changed, it is time for you to revise any decisions you have based on those facts.

THE EFFECT OF NEWS

Markets and various stocks can move dramatically for any number of reasons such as domestic events, international events, political reasons, and financial considerations. Just look at the news media and how they always have reasons underlying the news. The way they talk, you would think that journalists know everything, but in reality that is far from the truth. Even though their job is to report the news, in many instances these reporters think they are entertainers or analysts and many times create the news, whether inadvertently or not. Everything you see on television and read in the financial press may not be exactly and contextually correct. Mass media need "telling" stories every day in order to stay in business. A story may be embellished or slanted in order to be more alluring to the viewer or reader. The journalist may have omitted certain items or only reported upon events that confirmed the angle that the broadcaster wanted to exploit.

You should listen to what is being reported and try to balance the journalistic coverage with your own sense of logic. A good DAET trader understands this and does not react merely on the words of a media personality. For example, if a company is mentioned favorably by someone on CNBC, the reality is that the stock may move quickly. If a DAET trader decides to participate, the trader must understand that this move may be very short term and act accordingly. The trader may get in quickly with the intent of getting out almost immediately for a small fraction, or wait for the stock to go up and then short the stock when the all too often profit taking begins. The fact that the stock was mentioned on CNBC only meant that it could be in play for the next few minutes and not necessarily more than that.

As you follow analysts and commentators, you will develop your own read with respect to who is usually right and which sources are normally wrong. At any given time, you want to determine the assumptions and reasons underlying anyone's predictions. The prediction is not as important as the rationale behind the forecast.

You can follow the news on your computer by clicking on to a rolling report of financial news headlines. Chart 6-1 is a fragment of news headlines from March 4, 1998. Each item is time-dated in military-style time. The headline of the news article can be opened by the click of a mouse to display the entire news report. In my judgment the news is not as important as some traders think.

ANALYSIS OF FACTS

The factual story is not as important as the spin the analysts put on the facts. The market has performance expectations on

NEWS HEADLINES FROM VARIOUS WIRES

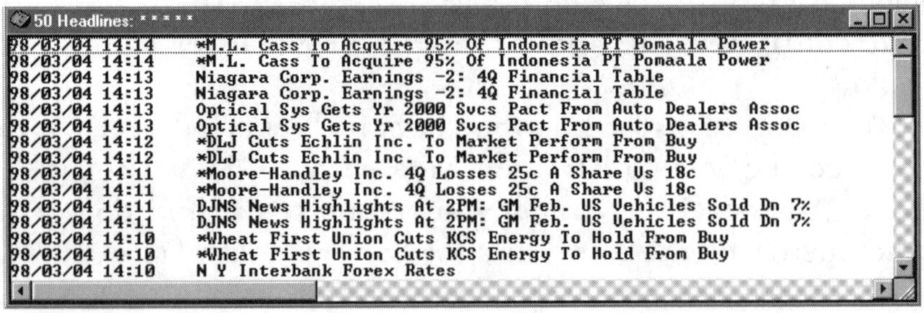

CHART 6-1. Some news headlines from March 4, 1998. The news is not as important as some traders believe.

the earnings and situation of each stock. Normally, you need to know what the expectations have been in order to understand whether those expectations have been exceeded or disappointed. If a stock earns $0.99 a share, is this good news or bad news? It all depends. If the market anticipated $0.82, then the news is good. If the market anticipated $1.01, then this could spell big trouble. Lately, anticipating stock directions after the reporting of earnings has been a relative crap shoot. Apparent good results can be interpreted as bad and bad results may be considered as good because there are so many "geniuses" and "experts" whispering so many "informed" numbers that no one really knows what is going on. Therefore, the direction of a stock after the release of earnings can be anyone's guess. My advice is to wait and see before chasing your tail after earnings are reported.

Some news is so obviously devastating that even the Three Stooges would recognize disaster; however, profiting from this type of news may be difficult because usually it is announced before the opening of trading or after the close. A gapped-down opening is most likely, perhaps a significant percentage of a stock's former price. For example, after negative news, Oxford Health Care opened down over half of the previous night's closing price. The trading decision at that point was whether one bought the stock at this level or shorted the stock in anticipation of further decline. It turns out that if you shorted Oxford, you would have been a significant winner, despite the fact that it had dropped so precipitously compared with its former price. This example illustrates why I usually recommend that traders go home flat. This type of excitement you don't need!

The opposite scenario can be just as true. News can be buoyant to stock prices. For example, merger announcements, takeovers, management changes, stock splits, big contract awards, FDA approvals, and other good news can spike up the price of a stock. Once again, however, most of these events are announced before the opening or after the close, and therefore the opportunity to trade within the move is remote. Most likely you will have to make a trading decision based upon the opening price, which will probably be significantly different from the previous close.

Sometimes what seems like an important news event may not affect the price of a stock as much as you thought it would because the news may very well have already been anticipated and is already reflected in the current market price for that stock. When this phenomenon occurs, it is said that the market has "discounted" the news in advance.

When I wake up in the morning, I watch the morning business news on TV. The most current news will be on TV but will not always be in the *Wall Street Journal,* which has been printed the night before. Incidentally, I normally watch CNBC. When I arrive in the office, I match the news with the preopening market-maker quotes in order to see how the news impacted the market. If a stock such as Intel reports that it may be lowering the price of its product, I want to see what impact this news will have on Intel and related stocks in the same industry, such as VSLI, NVLS, AMAT, and a variety of others.

I also check Reuters, the TV in the office, and the current ticker in order to see upgrades and downgrades of stock. I also study *Investor's Business Daily* in order to identify stocks breaking out or falling out of favor and the impact on any one stock or any group of stocks, because that is where the volatility in the opening prices in the Nasdaq market may occur. As I approach the market opening, I try to determine if my trading decision on these particular stocks is still appropriate. Generally, if a stock is priced significantly lower on the opening than I expect from my analysis of the news, I may be hesitant to follow a down direction. The reason is that the market makers may have lowered the stock so far that it may rebound in the next few minutes. The market makers may have so many sell orders in hand that they gap the stock dramatically lower in order to buy the shares at very opportunistic prices and resell them immediately to bargain hunters who come in shortly after the open.

In order to understand the psychology of the market, you must have some insight into crowd mass psychology. When the crowd hears news, many times it will react in a fairly predictable manner—and that is to overreact to the news. Market makers know this and play crowd behavior with the virtuosity of a philharmonic conductor. The Direct Access Electronic Trader can take advantage of crowd overreaction by reacting intelligently. You need to know that crowd behavior differs from individual behavior because while there is safety and anonymity in a crowd, individual decisions carry personal accountability. You can capitalize on mass psychology as long as you realize what is happening. Very often the time to buy stocks is when they have settled to about equilibrium after everyone else is tired of selling them. For example, when what is perceived to be bad news comes out, the market makers very often quote the opening price of stock much lower in order to buy the stock that the masses belch up out of fear. A rational view of the facts may determine that the stock should open 3 points lower. The market makers, however, will deliberately overreact and downtick the stock 5 points. The market makers, having many market sell orders in hand, will buy these shares at bargain basement prices on the opening and try to resell the stock they have purchased from the masses at the higher rational prices as soon as the market adjusts to reality. Baron Rothschild used to say that the time to buy was when blood is running in the streets. The time to sell is when you feel that you "gotta own 'em."

WHERE DO I FIND MY SIGNALS?

I am often asked about where a trader acquires market information triggering buy and sell signals. I answer that my personal trading decisions come from the momentum I spot on the various market quotation tickers, especially Nasdaq. This tape watching is so dominant a factor in selecting potential trading opportunities that I have developed a tracking program that monitors and sorts all Nasdaq stocks based upon criteria that I personally deem important. Your trading system should have a selective sorting program that sorts according to any criteria you wish, such as market-maker price changes, volume, spreads, number of market makers, and frequency of changes. This tracking system should be able to monitor the market the way you would want to if you had unlimited mental capacity.

It is physically impossible for a human being in one glance to observe all the movement and search through all the data on the over 5000 stocks trading on Nasdaq and to assimilate all the changes happening in the market. While your DAET system should include a computer program that will allow human beings to observe changes in the market and to react quickly to those changes based upon preprogrammed criteria, I am not an advocate of programmed trading. The Crash of 1987 was caused by programmed trading triggering other sell programs until the slide was so precipitous that no broker dared to answer the telephone.

Price information comes from two sources. One source is external to the market, and the other source arises from the inner workings of the price mechanism within the market. External information by definition is exogenous to the market and can be obtained by anyone. With due diligence and research time, we can all discover SEC filings, the worldwide need for any company's products, world news, and industry news. Usually, much outside information is available on the Internet. Every industry has its own professional publications spreading the gossip about personnel changes within the industry and management styles of leading chief executives. There is even a weekly dry cleaning magazine! In theory, all people have access to the research reports, evaluations, theories, and opinions of experts.

Internal price information was historically the exclusive province of market insiders. Until recently, even major exchanges would delay price quotes to the general public. Current stock prices were treated like CIA classified documents and not to be revealed to the general public for at least 15 minutes. Customers especially were deemed to have no need to know.

Internal price discovery was a two-tier system in which the inside professionals had more current price information than the "informationless" customer. In addition, insiders and institutions had access to secret markets where they conducted their own business at prices never reflected on Nasdaq. A major source of internal market information is recent price movement. This is why one trading axiom is that your last trade or most recent source of information is the genesis of your next trading decision. An entire school of theory believes that all the history of a stock is reflected in its current price. According to this theory the technical charts and the fundamental analysis of a company's future have all been reflected in the pricing mechanism.

STANDARD ANALYSIS

You will want to understand technical and fundamental analysis of stocks and markets. Remember that analysis of what happened in the past is an indicator of what may happen in the future—but it may not be relevant in the very short term of intraday trading, which is based upon seconds and minutes and not weeks, months, fiscal quarters, or years. In other words, your analysis may be superb, but the intraday market may not agree with your sense of timing. Understanding various valuation methods for predicting stock prices is not imperative for success at Direct Access Electronic Trading, but, like chicken soup, it can't hurt. A trader's education is a continuing process where self-improvement is better than self-stimulation.

TECHNICAL ANALYSIS

Technical analysis concerns price forecasting using methods based upon a study of price itself as opposed to the underlying fundamental (economic) market factors. Technical analysis is normally contrasted to fundamental analysis. Technical analysis looks at the interpretation of historical price charts in order to perceive support and resistance price levels from historical data. Direct Access Electronic Traders sometimes use technical analysis as a predictor of support and resistance levels. As a general rule, however, we are usually more interested in intraday price volatility and the tendency of prices to move in a given direction (either up or down) in a relatively short duration of time. We tend to subscribe to that market theory that states that all you need to know about a stock is reflected in its actual price from moment to moment.

The quote system any major DAET brokerage firm provides will produce charts and graphs of price movement over minutes, days, weeks, months, and years. Your trading system should also be able to publish real-time charts on all relevant indicators and even to superimpose one chart upon another. For example, if the index shows that the Nasdaq market is up 10 points, is this good news? You don't know until you know where the "up 10" came from. If the market had been up 20 points and was now only up 10, then the market is falling. The charts will give you a vivid picture and an instant grasp. An intraday chart can bring you up to date and "catch you up" with developments you may have missed.

Chart 6-2 contains two individual charts. The bottom chart is a picture of the Nasdaq 100 index for the day of March 4 displayed in 1-minute increments. You have already seen the ticker displaying the Nasdaq 100 stocks comprising the index in Chart 2-2. Note that the bottom chart in 6-2 is a graph while Chart 2-2 is a ticker. Any particular stock in the ticker (Chart 2-2) may or may not outperform the index pictured in the graph at the bottom of Chart 6-2.

The top box in Chart 6-2 superimposes a chart of Sun Microsystems, Inc., over the chart of the Nasdaq 100 index. By superimposing any stock chart over the Nasdaq 100 index chart you can better evaluate any stock's performance relative to the Nasdaq 100 index. Charts are extremely important until you have mastered trading techniques. Experienced traders are usually charting stocks in their head whether they realize it or not. They instinctively know the highs and the lows, levels of resistance and support, and other relevant data just as a homemaker knows sales prices of foodstuffs. The veteran DAET trader has no time to roll up a chart for a look-see because the trade is already gone by the time the chart can be read.

CHART 6-2. By superimposing any stock chart over the Nasdaq 100 index chart, you can better evaluate any stock's performance relative to the Nasdaq 100 index.

FUNDAMENTAL ANALYSIS

Fundamental analysis is the use of economic data to forecast prices. Fundamental analysis includes a great deal of research into the business and affairs of a company and its relative standing and strengths when compared with its competition and future prospects for the sale of its goods and services. You would, at the very least, investigate a company's sales, cash position and cash needs, competitor's product lines, sensitivity to changes in interest rates, and annual financial and cash flow statements.

If one is trading with market-maker techniques, there are times when fundamental analysis may become important to Direct Access Electronic Traders. If one is positioning shares, even for a short period of time, having a basic knowledge of the company's business makes sense. If one is trading as a momentum trader, however, fundamental analysis may prove more harmful than beneficial, because if the trader develops an opinion about the company, either good or bad, it may very well interfere with the fluid nature that the momentum trader must maintain in order to be effective. For example, if a trader believes that the fundamentals of Intel are excellent, selling it short may be a more difficult event even though this is what the market is telling the trader to do. Momentum traders should very rarely have opinions (fundamental) concerning the stocks they trade.

THE ACID TEST OF ANY TRADE

Direct Electronic Access Traders buy and sell all day. Even though they don't normally have to read any books on economics or annual reports, they are thinking and playing mental chess all day long. Intense concentration, total focus, and interrelationship of numbers occupy their work time. Traders do not need the mental ability to play 64 simultaneous games of chess blindfolded, but many of them, if challenged, could remember many prices in a supermarket in one pass. An orchestra conductor I know can remember 75 percent of an opera score in one reading, 95 percent in the second pass, and 100 percent forever on the third reading.

A trader need not possess such feats of memory. Many traders, however, can remember the support, resistance, and historical prices of 30 to 300 stocks with relative ease. I train neophyte traders to start with two stocks, feel how the stocks breathe, and then increase the traders' understanding to six stocks. New traders should trade slowly and deliberately. Adopt the motto of Augustus Caesar and "make haste slowly." Augustus was the last person to conquer the entire known occidental world (except Scotland). Trade slowly and learn, because your inventory of trades translates into profit and loss.

DAET involves being true to yourself. There is no percentage in cheating by not counting or deferring unrealized losses. Lying to yourself is like cheating on a diet. Any security in your inventory is worth what it is currently trading at, not what you bought it for or wish it were. Neither hope nor prayer will change the current market price. If a stock you own is down 1 point, it doesn't mean that it is more likely to go back up that point instead of down another. Trading decisions must be made on current market evaluation rather than the strength of your hopes and desires or religious beliefs.

Only three things can happen to a stock after you buy (sell) it:

1. It can go up.
2. It can go down.
3. It can stay the same.

Two of the three things that can happen to the stock are favorable or neutral to the trader. If the stock goes your way—*great!* If it stays the same—no problem—a minor inconvenience. If it goes against you, the more you let yourself lose, the worse it is. Simple, isn't it?

Recognizing that the market has turned against your position is the right thing to do because you must stop your loss before the loss becomes a costly mistake. You don't buy a position to get lucky. You don't take shots at the market hoping to hit a bull's-eye. Save your prayers for more important events than the short-term movement of the price of a stock.

Making miscalls is part of the game. Let's assume that you want to travel to Boston and you mistakenly jump on the wrong train, which is headed to Washington, D.C. How long would you remain on this train? Are you going to stay on Amtrak all the way to Washington or are you going to get off at the first stop. The same philosophy applies to taking your losses.

To take no action is in itself an action. This sounds like mystical philosophy, but it is a truism. If you take no action with respect to a losing position, you have chosen to maintain the status quo, which in itself is an action. You will then reap the consequences of this action. To be successful, you must have the gumption to execute an essential loss-control maneuver. Everyone has or will develop an individual trading style. Regardless of that style, discipline must be maintained.

I cannot say enough about the importance of discipline in order to be a successful trader. When real estate moguls reveal the secrets of making millions in real estate, the three secrets are always location, location, location. The reason is that keystone real estate usually keeps its relative value. In Direct Access Electronic Trading the secret is discipline, discipline, discipline.

I could recite a great number of platitudes like "Your first loss is your smallest," "Health makes wealth," and "Early to bed, early to rise." None of these self-truths is eternally valid because there is always an equal and opposite adage to counter the first maxim. Take your pick. For example, "Should one act in haste and repent at leisure," or "Does the early bird get the worm?" In truth and in fact, *the eternal discipline in trading is to cut your loss prudently.* If the market turns adverse, you must take your loss or scratch a trade. No ifs, ands, or buts. No maybes and no praying. Just fold the hand like you would any bad hand in poker.

Once a decision turns adverse, any more money or time invested in pursuit of rescuing that decision is a vanity that you cannot afford. You are then preoccupying your concentration and populating your life with lose-lose decisions instead of pursuing winning strategies. There is nothing personal about the situation. The market doesn't know you and doesn't care how you feel. So don't take losses personally. If the market turns adverse, it has nothing to do with you as an individual.

I know that my advice to cut your losses immediately appears to conflict with my other advice about being a parameter trader and holding a losing position a tad longer than normal in order to avoid being wiggled and jiggled out. Both pieces of advice are reconcilable because each is appropriate at different points on your learning curve. At the beginning of your DAET career it's best to take your losses quickly for purposes of discipline and control, because you won't have the product knowledge to identify the reasons behind the adverse price movement. The freshman DAET trader won't be able to distinguish a wiggle from a waggle so I advise keeping your ammunition (capital) preserved until you can discern irrational price movements (head fakes).

If there is any one concept in this book that is important for you to remember and will help you the most throughout your trading life, this is it. This is my major test for successful Direct Access Electronic Trading:

> **If I didn't already own (short) my position, would I do it now?**

Ask yourself this question over and over again after you have established a position. This is what I call mentally "marking your position to market." Just because you already own or are already short a position does not mean that's the way it must be. Optimally a trader should have positions that reflect his or her current belief about where the market is *now* going. Just because you have a position doesn't mean that you should hold it.

This acid test is applied on an ongoing basis to each position you have. In theory, you want to continually ask yourself this question when you have positions in your inventory. You would be like a computer constantly scanning and analyzing your criteria for maintaining your positions.

Keep concentrating on the answer to this question. Focus on the question as a mantra until the chant becomes synchronous with your heartbeat. The phrase should become as ingrained as a religious incantation. Recite the question "If I didn't own my position, would I own it now?" until it becomes a part of your trading persona. If you give yourself an honest answer to this question, you will cut your losses immediately when a trade turns against you. You will also evaluate your gains and decide whether to ring the cash register or let your profits ride—until the next time you answer the question of ultimate truth.

A common and highly erroneous theory is that traders in a profit position are trading "with the market's money." Nothing could be further from the truth. The profit is real money and belongs to the trader and not to the market. There is no such thing in trading as the "market's money". For example, if you bought a stock at $82 per share and the stock has risen to $86 per share, that $4 profit belongs to you, not to the market.

Mark your positions to market price all the time and consider your profits to be real money. Do not wind up with paper profits that turn into real losses. Conversely, losses are painful and should normally not be deferred overnight. If you hold a position overnight, you are hoping to become lucky instead of relying upon your trading skills. If you feel lucky, you can always buy the stock on opening in the morning without running an additional risk of overnight price declines.

We live in a world awash with uncertainty and molting with change. Everything changes every day, and we adjust to change in every way. Price changes in the Nasdaq stock market are the changes we want to capitalize upon. The twin terrors of uncertainty and change force us to make midcourse corrections to our original flight plan. If you make a trade and the market does not go your way, you must adjust your trading position in order to attenuate the market risk. Always be prepared to reexamine each trading decision immediately after you have made the decision and while you are living with the consequences. Furthermore, always be prepared to change a previous decision when you are confronted with new facts.

RARELY HOLD OVERNIGHT POSITIONS

It is my personal belief that *Direct Access Electronic Traders should rarely, if ever, take home overnight positions.* Some other DAET firms preach a different gospel and encourage traders to take overnights. I recommend that you avoid overnight positions until you have mastered enough trading skills to do the right thing. My many years of DAET have led me to the generalization that you should not allow the market to force you to take an overnight position, but you might consider an overnight if you truly believe that carrying the position home is being done because of a high probability of additional profit rather than because you want to avoid taking your loss now.

Usually a trader takes home overnight positions only because the trader refuses to accept the immediate loss. In my experience, a trader's reluctance to take a quick loss usually results in greater losses and many times can spell disaster for the trader. A small loss soon becomes a large one, and the trader becomes even more reluctant to take the loss. This prescription for disaster has a tendency to feed on itself until the trader may very well be driven out of the business.

My point is that traders should never fight the market. By going home "flat," the DAET trader has a sure mechanism for never having an adverse price movement take that trader by surprise during the night. This is truer today than ever before because now most major news releases concerning stocks are reported after the close or before the opening, thereby increasing the potential risk of an overnight calamity.

Perhaps the worst problem created by taking home positions that go against the trader is that while suffering the loss (which is bad enough), traders have a tendency to stop constructive trading that would generate profitable trades. Don't put yourself in a position where you are licking your wounds instead of being constructive. Continuing aggregating losses is a terrible situation that will sap your attention and can overwhelm your otherwise good judgment.

On rare occasions one might take a position that is really working out well and have the desire to retain that trade overnight because the momentum remains intact going into the close. This is the only case in which I will grudgingly concede that taking home a position might make sense. For example, suppose one buys COMS at 33, by the close of trading it has risen to $36^{1}/_{2}$, it seems to be closing very strongly, and the trader wants to hold it overnight because of a belief that it will open even higher. I might be persuaded to concur that this is an acceptable choice, especially if it does open higher the next day.

I have been monitoring traders for years, and I can unequivocally say:

> **There is no percentage in taking home overnight trading positions. Don't do it!**

Even if you are occasionally right, in the long run overnight positions are usually net losses and cause anxiety and pressure that may affect your next-day trading activities. You don't need this kind of aggravation, so don't do it. *No overnights—get it!*

QUESTION: What is the definition of an investment?

ANSWER: A trade that went bad.

Under *no* circumstances let your bad trades become your future. If you do, you are relying on investing rather than on trading skill. The decision processes of an investor and a trader are different. When you invest in a stock, you are looking for intrinsic value and anticipated future performance of the issuer over a long period of time. In DAET you are looking to capitalize on the intraday movements in stock prices.

Investing is a permissible and legitimate activity. The business of America is business, and I encourage you to invest in and for your future. You may invest as much as you wish, but don't allow adverse trades to become your retirement portfolio. This is the rationale behind my "no overnight positions" rule, which is an automatic mechanism for preventing the very human desire to avoid financial pain by postponing a loss.

SELLING SHORT

The American way is to invest for the long term. Most American investors are investing for the long-term future and are buying on the expectation that the stock market will continue to go up. It doesn't take genius to make money in a bull market where stocks are going up independently of any action that any one trader or investor is taking. A bull market can cover a universe of trading sins.

In a short sale, the trader or investor is selling stock that the investor or trader does not own in the expectation that the stock price will drop. Many people have never understood the concept of selling short. In effect, the short seller is selling a stock that he or she doesn't own in anticipation of a decrease in the price of that stock. The hope is that if the stock goes down, the seller will be able to replace the shares at a lower price and the price differential will be the profit. Conversely, if the price increases, the short seller will be forced to pay up for the stock, thus incurring a loss. The average investor does not often sell short because of an inbred belief that it is wrong to sell something you don't own. Short sellers theoretically face unlimited loss because there is no limit to how high a stock price can go, whereas a long buyer can never lose more than the purchase price. If you short (sell) a stock at 10 and the price rises to over 100, you will lose more than 90 points, but if you went long (bought) the stock at 10 and it went to zero, all you lost was 10 points.

Only a robber baron like Jay Gould could finagle himself into a position where he shorted (sold) more shares than were available for repurchase in the market in an attempt to buy control of Commodore Vanderbilt's railroad. Gould was forced to buy the last share from the commodore at rich, arterial blood prices. Hence, the ditty that "he who sells what isn't hisen, must deliver or go to prison."

The professional trader is far more sophisticated than the average investor and knows that selling short is just as legitimate a trading strategy as going long. In order to make money trading, you must sell a stock for more than you bought it. It doesn't matter whether you buy or sell (short) the stock first, as long as you wind up selling it for more than it cost.

Often, when the price of a stock rises, it increases slowly due to incremental profit taking. When a stock price decreases, however, it often drops quickly in a very pronounced and recognizable manner. Traders want to be positioned to take advantage of a drop in the price of a stock because there are fewer people able to take advantage of the opportunity.

THE NEW WALL STREET NINJA

Today's successful DAET trader will not typically make a large profit on any single trade. Rather, the DAET trader will flip in and out of the same security or market-sector security over and over during the same market move. A recent Nasdaq rule change makes clear that traders may reinitiate the same side of the same security at will so long as their current position is flat.

For example, it is unlikely that a great trader will buy SUNW at 28 and hold it during a move to 32 (if that move occurred intraday), making a 4-point profit. It is much more likely that the trading would look like this:

BOT....	28	
SOLD...	$28^3/8$.....	$+^3/8$
BOT....	$28^1/2$	
SOLD...	$28^3/4$......	$+^1/4$
BOT....	29	
SOLD...	$29^1/2$.....	$+^1/2$
BOT....	$29^5/8$	
SOLD...	$30^3/8$....	$+^3/4$
BOT....	$30^3/4$	
SOLD...	$31^1/2$....	$+^3/4$
BOT....	$31^3/4$	
SOLD...	32......	$+^1/4$
BOT....	32	
SOLD...	$31^3/4$......	$-^1/4$
Total profit		$2^5/8$
Total tickets		14

Although the total profit is lower than the theoretical 4-point gain, this scenario is very real and obtainable, with the trader continuously returning to a neutral position, thereby avoiding significant loss if and when the market finally reverses. The trader remains in control and prepared to change direction on a moment's notice—*no home run BUT consistent trading profitability.*

Real happiness in DAET stems from a trading style favoring consistency. It is probably healthier for you to have a sweet procession of profitable trading days instead of nineteen days of losses followed one big gorging day in which you make a huge profit. Consistency is the mark of a true professional in any field of endeavor. It is far better for a baseball team to hit four straight singles instead of one home run. Every sport maintains its own set of statistics such as RBIs, ERAs, on-base percentages, foul line percentages, and the like. The purpose of the statistics is to predict what any given player will do in any given situation against any other player.

Most people prefer consistency and predictability in human behavior instead of chaos. While you can trade like a lunatic as long as you are making money, you should develop your own trading style that suits your individual personality and outlook. My advice to you is not to look for the home runs. Lead the league in on-base percentage. Consistency is a virtue.

Any trader who holds a position for 4 points without trading in and out will most likely hold a loss of 14 points. Make less, but be consistent and safe—turn over your positions often, and stay liquid by returning to neutral. *Take losses as readily as you are willing to take profits.* Take the profit that the market will give you. It is best in the very short term if you take a position based upon a trend and close out that position while the same trend is still in intact.

Recovering to no position prepares you to jump on the next opportunity—whatever that may be—whatever stock, whatever side (long or short), without agonizing over hurtful situations with accompanying emotional stress. This sense of balance is relied upon by any great athlete. You pick the sport and I'll bet on this technique. Any great tennis player hits the ball and immediately returns to the middle of the court (neutral) unless the anticipated return shot will have to be placed elsewhere. With balance and anticipation, in both tennis and trading, you know that the next shot has great promise of being a winner.

Successful DAET traders are no longer the Robin Hoods of Wall Street but have evolved into Wall Street ninjas. Ninjas are Japanese commandos, who have historically been skilled in the art of watching an enemy and exploiting weakness through stealth and silence. Ninjas adapt to circumstances and excel in discipline. Traders can learn the ninja art of watching, absorbing, adapting, and prevailing by adhering to sheer discipline.

MARKET-MAKER SECRETS

Market makers know that DAET traders account for approximately 20 percent of the daily trading volume on Nasdaq. Market makers know that DAET traders desire, on balance, to go home flat and thus have no staying power for any great period of time because of their need to close out positions by the end of the trading day. Therefore market makers want to wiggle and jiggle prices during the day in order to shake out DAET traders before the end of the day. It is interesting to note that market makers also, on balance, like to flatten out their positions by the end of the day and quote more competitive prices nearer the close. At least one recent study by Professors Simaan and Whitcomb indicates that market makers become much more competitive in their prices when they want to close out their trading inventory at the end of every day. I have only seen a draft of this study, but the results should be further explored by the trader and taken into account when trading near the end of the day.

The market close is perhaps the best time of the day for exploiting trading opportunities. Volume generally rises, price movements intensify, and opportunities abound. You could extract from the Simaan-Whitcomb study referred to above that market-maker wiggles and jiggles are less frequent when trading the close. Be sure to keep a clear head and be aggressive, but remember, I do not advise Direct Access Electronic Traders to take home positions; so, therefore, only enter into positions that you will be able to close out before the close of the trading day. Remember that *overnight positions,* on balance, spell *disaster.*

In addition, trading styles cannot be cast in stone and must be modified from time to time in order to keep them effective in changing market conditions. Your education is never complete, in that nuances and correlations that work today may be worthless tomorrow. Also, the market is always changing, so that you enter the same river but the currents and the water are different every time.

SECTOR TRADING

A trader eventually develops a list of companies that participate in the same industry and in the same line of business. The assumption is that if the news bashes or bolsters the stock of a particular market leader in any given industry, there may be a correlative spillover effect on stocks of other companies whose product lines are substantially similar. This cascading effect has two consequences.

First, the relative strength or weakness of any bellwether stock may act as a barometer for the remaining stocks in that sector. Your sense of anticipation may allow you to begin trading on the trend before the trend is noticed by anyone else. It depends on how many price movements you need to recognize as the beginning of a trend. Some chartists believe that increasing prices, which do not break a top line, already constitute a downward trend. Others need more confirmation.

Also, second and third-tier lower-cap stocks are generally lower priced than the more highly priced, well-capitalized market leaders. These lower prices of the lower-tier stocks often allow you to keep this kind of position open within your margin availability while you are trading other stocks.

Continuing refinement of the product-line matches adds exactness and lack of distortion to the forecasting potential of your sector list. You must also make adjustments from time to time to your industry chart so that you compare peer groups and their associations relative to market swings. Verify whether the second- and third-tier companies in that industry are moving in tandem with price changes, as you would expect, and evaluate the synergies. In general, it is a valid assumption to presume that similarly situated companies in the same field will react in unison to the impact of both good and bad news.

You will have no problem in developing and refining your own sector list.

DON'T CONFUSE A BULL MARKET FOR BRAINS

One of my objections to the short-sale rule, which allows shorts only on an uptick on the bid side, is the bloating consequences that a long-term bias gives to the stock market. Pension funds, money managers, and investors have enormous amounts of capital and, as a rule, are buying the market's upside potential. Most people in the world have heard that stocks "keep up with inflation" and are the so-called best long-term mechanism for investing in general. The result is general market price inflation because more money is chasing a limited supply of stocks.

Many of today's most successful portfolio managers have been reared in a raging bull market where stocks have steadily risen in price. These managers have never lived through a bear market where stock prices drop day after day until suicide seems like a viable and natural option. One of DAET's major appeals to traders is that they can make money in a down market as well as in an uptrend.

I have often been quoted as saying that most professional traders make most of their money in bear markets because stock price reversals are clear and dramatic. A flagrant bull market may only have a dozen great bear market days in a year, but one day's bear market profit can put a child through a year of college. As a DAET trader, you should take whatever gains the market is willing to give to you. Take all those incremental rises in the price of a stock. But also position yourself and prepare yourself to sell short if and when the market is dropping.

Real traders are always waiting for a "bad" (down) stock market day. The rest of the world is waiting for a "good" (up) stock market day. Isn't it great to know that, as a trader, you have opportunities every day? The only "bad" day you will ever have is when you lose money, irrespective of what the market is doing. DAET provides a natural and easy hedge for your other investments. Don't be dissuaded by long-term recommendations to buy 1000 shares of MSFT and sleep for 20 years like Rip Van Winkle.

When the stock market is rising, it does not take brains to make a long-term investment that increases in value. Don't believe that good investments in a bull market are necessarily a sign of competence.

Many traders make trades in as few as two or three different stocks in which they believe they have developed a special expertise. These traders watch every movement these stocks make and try to determine why the stock has moved and what the stock will do in the immediate future. These traders have followed these stocks over a long period of time and feel they know everything there is to know about price movement and the major market makers in those stocks.

When you begin trading, you should focus on no more than a small number of stocks in the beginning until you secure a "feel" for the stocks and familiarization with their cycles. The hope is that you will grasp an understanding of their trading orbits.

MARKET-MONITORING PROGRAMS

Sophisticated trading programs can actively monitor price movement on the Nasdaq Level II system so traders can act on that movement in a split second. Your DAET firm should have a market-monitoring program that allows DAET traders to establish individualized search parameters that will direct the computer system to continually scan the Nasdaq market and notify the trader of any prescribed movement. Your trading program acts like a robot burglar alarm with motion detectors. The monitoring program identifies trends based upon whatever indicators the individual DAET trader deems important. The market-monitoring programs can be customized to suit any individual's trading style. For example, these programs will search for trade candidates based upon price, volume, spread, volatility, and any other indicators the individual trader wishes to see. It is physically impossible for any trader to watch the more than 5000 companies trading on Nasdaq. The market-monitoring programs act as your second set of eyes and ears. This alert will be your version of the Star Wars early detection system. I don't see how anyone can trade without this feature.

DAET increases trading volume and creates intraday liquidity. The whole idea of the market is to allow traders, investors, and other participants to buy and sell easily. You don't care why anyone else is a trader, or investor, or speculator. All you want is liquidity so that you as a trader have someone to take the other side of your transaction. DAET is thousands of traders who create liquidity, while the market makers are there to steal and stuff their pockets at the expense of the telephone-ordering, e-mailing investing public.

TRADING TIPS

Every good trader develops a grab bag of devices, which work as so-called leading trading indicators. These trading indicators are the keys that predict a potential trading opportunity. These indicators are based upon factors that have worked for this trader in the past. Accordingly, the trader is looking to trade on these keys whenever they line up sequentially. Good traders are not usually willing to disclose their trading keys. They don't want to release their treasure map to the general public any more than you would want to reveal the tricks of the family business to a nonfamily member.

I am basically a man of action. I am an activist. You cannot grab opportunity unless you are prepared to take action. The merry-go-round is always spinning, but you must have the initiative to reach for the brass ring. My advice is always to be decisive. Prepare for the worst and hope for the best, but *do something*. Otherwise, you become embroiled in what the economist Milton Friedman called the "tyranny of the status quo." One of life's major problems is overcoming inertia. A body at rest tends to stay at rest until moved.

The orders you miss are the orders you really want. We all get greedy and expect to buy at the absolute bottom and sell at the very all-time high. Wake up and get real! Your best chances of success are to turn your position during the middle of the trend line. I mean that you want to initiate a trading position when the stock is moving and close out the position while the stock is still moving in the same direction. Once the price reverses, you are sinking in quicksand, and anyone who buys your position may be standing on your shoulders.

Moreover, don't let eighths of a point stand in the way of a profit. Chances are that a position that looked good at an eighth may still be a good trade when it is moving to a quarter. If we all waited to buy at the high and sell at the low, the market would crawl to a halt.

When you make a profit, you did something right. Don't be a crybaby and feel that you left money on the table because you did not sell at the very high for the day, week, month, or year. You can always return to that stock. You can acquire another stock that is moving your way. There is always another cookie in the supermarket and another trade in the stock market. There will be another bus in 10 minutes.

Don't spend the rest of the day crying over the DAET equivalent of cookie crumbs. Think healthy and look for new trading opportunities. The most successful traders trade actively and don't even think about what could have happened as they trade. Don't agonize about what has happened. Go with the flow of the market.

Never look back in Anguish!
Always look forward for additional opportunities.

NOT EVERY TRADE WILL GO YOUR WAY EVERY TIME

There is a difference between a good trade that didn't go your way and a bad trade. Market forces are beyond your capability to control, and you may have been absolutely right in your judgment about a trade but slightly off in your sense of timing. Sometimes, you can be too smart. I usually attribute the failure of the market to change my way to the failure of other market participants to see what I see. There is a strong adherence to the pleasure and pain principal in DAET. I assume that everyone trades for the rational reason of maximizing capital by either capturing profit or preventing loss.

Every trade confirms a mutual understanding of value. One party buys what another sells. And both are happy, because most items are underpriced to the extent that no one parts with anything of value for something of less value. When the market fails to react according to my preconceptions, the irrationality may be due to head fakes, jiggles, bona fide timing differences, or a totally unrelated consideration. If you are fundamentally correct in your perception of a stock, you hope everyone else will recognize what you have already perceived.

A special pain will shred your heart when (1) you are right fundamentally and technically, (2) the trade should have been profitable, and (3) the trade actually was profitable in a longer time frame than you initially projected. It always hurts to lose money for the wrong reasons.

Always remember that a missed opportunity is not a lost opportunity. Chalk up the information you failed to act upon to the increase of your learning curve. The next time you see the same situation, you are poised for profit. *Never look back and cry!*

TRADE WITH ZEST!

Most DAET traders would rather trade than do anything else, except maybe eat or procreate. DAET traders love to trade and, consequently, look forward to each trading day. Entering into the trading arena to a trader is like putting on the glimmering suit of lights to a bullfighter. Trading gives the thrill and acceleration of taking off in a Lear jet which is so powerful that it rises straight up like a rocket. Traders love anything to do with the market. They search endlessly for leading indicator relationships that will predict market trends. They never tire of doing research and hearing about the market.

DAET traders would rather trade than stay home. In fact, most traders hate a three-day weekend. I read somewhere that General Colin Powell, the former chairman of the Joint Chiefs of Staff, used to have a sign on his desk that proclaimed, "Thank God for Mondays." This burning desire to be in the office is the same mentality that draws traders to the market. If you don't enjoy what you are doing, you should most assuredly find another career. If you are dedicating seven hours a day each day of your life to a job that you really don't like, life can be a terrible waste. Your sense of boredom and general despair will flow over and corrupt your private life, which is too precious not to enjoy. I don't want to sound like a beer commercial, but you should grab all the gusto you can.

The whole point is that watching real traders in action is like watching a shark feeding frenzy. Traders are so caught up in trading that the day sails by effortlessly. Even when the trading day is over, real traders want to stay and discuss the market. They want to tell and retell old trading stories like Greek myths. Even professional athletes, from time to time, want to take time off from their training schedule, but traders cannot wait for the market to open.

MARKET OPENING TRADING STRATEGIES

On balance, I do not recommend that beginning DAET traders commit heavily during the first few minutes of the opening of the market. Very often the market is not very directional on the opening, and so it's best that unseasoned traders wait a bit before attempting to identify trends and putting their capital at risk.

Many considerations must be factored into the decision to commit early in the trading day. Among them are:

1. News events, including earnings reports released after the previous day's close or before the opening

2. Analyst upgrades and downgrades

3. Credit market conditions

4. Strength or weakness in the dollar

5. Overseas markets activity (Japan, England, France, Germany)

6. Commodities prices (precious metals)

7. General market sentiment

All of the above factors can influence opening prices. Remember that market makers usually try to exaggerate moves and play off your emotions—greed and fear. If good news (or whatever is perceived to be good news) is announced, the market makers intentionally move up opening prices far beyond realistic levels, hoping to suck in overanxious day traders. Conversely, bad news may very well be exaggerated by the market makers' precipitous markdowns on the opening. Many times an astute trader must sell a strong opening or buy a weak opening in order to profit significantly. Remember, *tread easy on market openings.*

It goes without saying that you should relate yesterday's closing price to the supervening events as you watch the market makers fix the opening prices up or down based upon their assessment of a particular stock and the market.

Usually, the hours of 1100 to 1400 (Nasdaq enters trades in military time), which translates to 11 a.m. to 2 p.m. for us civilians, are the slow times in day trading. This does not mean that there is no opportunity to make money. It just means that the volatility and velocity of trading volume slow down; more wiggles, jiggles, and head fakes are experienced; and trading sometimes becomes more difficult. Never trade out of boredom. There is no more unnecessary practice than trading because you have nothing else to do. I always advise traders to remain focused even when the market slows down, because you never know when a market opportunity will stand up on its rear legs and beg to be taken. It is important to maintain a state of alertness so you will be able to act instantly when events so demand. Losing concentration can cause hesitation when making a trading decision, and even a hiccup of indecisiveness can cost you a good trade. Don't be lazy—stay focused on task—if you don't, there are many others who will, and they will beat you to the punch every time.

NEVER AVERAGE DOWN

Averaging down is *death* to the DAET trader! For our purposes, price averaging consists of adding to a losing position after the price has dropped. The concept of dollar price averaging works over the long run, but *not* in the DAET environment. With dollar price averaging you buy 100 shares at $40 a share and another 100 shares when the stock has dropped to $20 a share; you have now reduced your average price per share to $30. To the long-term investor, this lower blended price is a benefit.

To the DAET trader, the price drop is a bad investment if you were long (because the price dropped from $40 to $30). This was a good stock to have shorted all the way down, but not a stock to have held an increasing position in as it fell.

In Direct Access Electronic Trading there should normally be no term longer than the close of today's market. If a stock is going down, gauge its potential again tomorrow morning when you see it going down even further. DAET traders are not trading for the long term because, as John Maynard Keynes noticed, we are all dead in the long term.

TRADING TIPS—NO FANCY STRADDLES ARE NECESSARY

Direct Access Electronic Trading is a WYSIWYG system: *What you see is what you get.* It is not necessary to study the spots off any book, or to absorb and understand complicated mathematical formulas promulgating fancy year-end straddles, butterfly straddles, and other complicated trading techniques. While many of these ideas look good on the drafting board, they normally work only in theory. In point of fact, complicated option and alternative market strategies are difficult for the average person to establish at profitable spreads. Since the DAET trader is only taking a small position for a relatively short duration of time, there is normally no need to seek fancy but impractical positions geared for the long-term investor or trader.

Success in trading comes from internal beliefs in concepts such as detachment, patience, avoidance of loss, and discipline. There is no complicated system other than the market is going up (down) so I will buy (sell); or the market has gone up (down) far enough so I will sell (buy). The business of DAET is basically straightforward. You must sell at a higher price than you buy.

Many people ask me, "How many trades should I do each day?" This question is akin to how many pages are there in a book or how long is a rope? The number of trades you should do each day will depend upon your personality and abilities and be dictated by market opportunities. When you first begin, 10 round-trip trades a day may be enough. As you become more proficient, you will want to increase your number of trades. In order to objectify trading potential, the market opens at 9:30 a.m. and closes at 4 p.m. This totals only 390 minutes a day available for trading. My best trader once did about 420 trades in one day. Just for the record he was able to average about a quarter of a point of profit per trade and he earned about $87,000 for the day. This is a very active level of trading which is highly unusual today.

As I said above, for the first few weeks, you most certainly should focus on one or two of the most liquid high-cap, widely traded stocks. A good trader can trade off the tape on about 12 stocks at one time.

The best trades are sometimes the trades that you missed. The reason is that many others also wanted those trades and someone just beat you to them. Ask any fisherman about the fish that got away.

ASPECTS OF A GOOD TRADER

A good trader is like a gunslinger in the old West. In addition to that hard, flinty glance, a professional trader needs discipline, concentration, discipline, an ability to remember numbers, discipline, and an ability to see patterns. Did I mention discipline?

I cannot mention discipline enough. The main discipline is to take your losses early. Never agonize over small losses. They are part of the trading game and living proof of your continuing discipline.

Concentration means the ability to look at ticker quotes and discern price movement and trends without letting anything distract you. Focus on the movement of the prices displayed on your trading screen. Also watch the trends on the market indexes.

THE MARKETMINDER SCREEN

The MarketMinder is a separate window that you can program to follow indexes and trends on your trading screen. A sample MarketMinder window is shown in Chart 6-3.

Your trading system will produce almost any index that you would reasonably want to see. The number of indexes is limited only by the bundled services that your quote provider can access.

In Chart 6-3 under the "Symbol" column you are watching several important indexes including the Dow Jones industrial index ($INDU), the Nasdaq composite index ($COMPX), the

MARKET MINDER

Symbol	Last		Change
DOW JONES INDUSTRIAL → $INDU	8504.12	↓	-80.71 ← THIS MEANS THE DOW JONES INDUSTRIAL AVERGAGE IS DOWN 80.71 FOR THE DAY
NASDAQ COMPOSITE INDEX → $COMPX	1751.73	↑	-5.41
NASDAQ 100 INDEX → $NDX	1171.88	↑	-3.84
US 30 YR TREASURY FUTURE → /USH8	119^15	↓	+^10
S&P 500 INDEX FUTURE → /SPH8	1045.90	↑	-9.70
S&P 500 CASH INDEX → $SPX	1043.92	↑	-8.10
SUN MICROSYSTEMS → SUNW	46 1/16	↓	+3/4

THE SYSTEM WILL GENERATE MOST INDEXES WHICH YOU WOULD WANT TO SEE

CHART 6-3. The Market Minder.

Nasdaq 100 index ($NDX), the U.S. 30-year Treasury bond future index (/USH8), and the S&P 500 cash index ($SPX). You can also watch the price of any stock you desire, such as Sun Microsystems (SUNW).

The second column in the MarketMinder chart is entitled "Last" because it reflects the last price. Between the "Last" column and the "Change" column is a directional arrow that shows green on the up arrow (increase) and red on the down arrow (decrease).

The "Change" column shows the plus or minus change for the day. Both the "Last" and the "Change" columns are color-coded green for increase and red for decrease. This is what I call the "Christmas tree."

The ability to remember numbers and note rapidly changing prices is integral to success. Great traders can trade off the ticker tape and ECNs by remembering the quoted bid and offer prices of every important market maker on most of the stocks they are trading. This ability to focus on moving numbers is a God-given gift. It is a combination of good eyes and good memory, which may translate into dollars by ringing the cash register early and often. Today, however, computers can assist people who have been neglected by God as to this innate gift.

SELECTION OF STOCKS IS IMPORTANT

Many DAET traders are advisedly expanding their horizon to stocks other than the highly capitalized, higher-priced, and more widely held top 100 Nasdaq darlings. As more and more people come into DAET, they may not want to compete with the talented veteran traders and the most resourceful market makers who tend to trade these stocks on a more active basis.

Accordingly, newer traders may want to specialize their trading in less trafficked stocks. There is significant volatility in thinly traded issues that have come into prominence in the market over the past few years. While this can be a good opportunity for trading profits, the characteristic of these smaller-cap stocks is to show choppier price movement with far less real trading volume. If you are right, you can be very right; but if you are wrong, it can be a disaster.

DAET is now becoming a mainstream occupation. Since my last book, DAET traders have been fruitful and multiplied. The ranks of people participating in DAET have increased exponentially, now numbering into the thousands, whereas just over a couple of years ago the total number might have been only a few hundred. I believe the size of the DAET trading community will be tens of thousands by the turn of the century. Over the next few years DAET will become a desired and chosen profession, and traders will evolve into the de facto market makers of the future by bidding and offering in between the spread.

In the past year, the proliferation of DAET traders has significantly changed the ways in which DAET traders must think. The participants, many of whom are following the same group of stocks, often place identical orders at or about the same time in securities that seem to be moving in one direction or another. The multiplicity and speed at which these orders are placed often cause a DAET trader to have to pay up or sell down from the price the trader believed was the price at the moment the order was entered. For example, if six market makers were bidding for Microsoft at $117^3/8$, and the perception was that the stock was about to go down because one or more market makers reduced their bid, it is not unusual for a dozen or more orders to sell the stock to come literally within a second or two. Accordingly, your choice of stocks is important and your preferences will also affect your intraday margin requirements.

The markets are far more competitive, more volatile, and more challenging than ever. No one knows what the trading market of the future will look like or how it will fully develop. I have my own ideas about how the market should operate and will share my view of the future with you. From the beginning I viewed DAET like President John F. Kennedy considered space during the Sputnik era—"a new ocean, and I believe the United States must sail upon it."

Among the events that have transpired over the last few years are the skyrocketing of the Dow, huge increases in other key indexes, and the ballooning of stock trading volume to unprecedented levels. The change of mass psychology concerning investments in general is leading to a massive restructuring of the equities market. An enormous amount of mutual fund money is locked into retirement funds. As today's baby boomers plan for retirement, the stock markets appear to be overbought. I believe that retirement fund money is supporting the stock markets and is not about to run to other investments. This support augers well for using DAET to trade the volatility. This "bloat" also affords short-selling opportunities for DAET as profit taking occurs.

Federal task forces are studying various methods of funding Social Security in the future. The Social Security pyramid will have fewer people supporting an aging population. Currently, the U.S. government invests your Social Security contributions in its own very long term bonds, which have no investment risk but repay with inflated dollars. One of the solutions proposed by the task forces is that Social Security be allowed to invest in the stock market (which has historically kept up with inflation) instead of fixed governmental obligations. This should result in added stimulus for the market as even more money chases the same stocks.

The Asian markets are in turmoil, and Asian investors may well look to the American stock market for stability and growth. With this as a backdrop it is necessary to understand what this new environment means to you and what opportunities can be derived from the current situation and the changes that are imminent. In my opinion, Direct Access Electronic Trading will palpably affect every exchange within a few years. Specialists on all exchanges are in jeopardy of losing their privileges just as the NASD market makers are losing theirs. In this regard, a recent FBI sting operation uncovered major front-running operations on the NYSE.

When volatility is high and price movements are significant in stocks, it really doesn't matter how *many* people are trading as long as *you* make money. You shouldn't care about the number of players; the only thing that matters to you is how much you can capitalize on this volatility. For example, if you see Apple Computer starting to move, buy it, and make one-half of a point, does it really matter to you how many other people have capitalized on the same situation? In fact, the bigger the game gets, the better the game gets as more players create more liquidity and opportunity because of their diversity of interest. You shouldn't care what anyone else is doing as long as your trade can be executed at the price you want.

In fact, the greatest advantage of DAET is that it guarantees an individual liquidity. No longer does a trader have to worry about being able to sell or buy. The trader's only worry is whether he or she is on the right or wrong side of the market. DAET is growing every day and can continue to accommodate growth. Like Robin Hood's band of merry men, the more the merrier.

MATHEMATICAL TRADING LOSS PARAMETERS

I don't believe in setting mathematical trading loss parameters.

Some believe that a trader should establish numerical ranges, which guide trading losses. This highly erroneous theory suggests that a trader should determine to accept a certain loss limit each day and cease trading after the limit has been reached.

If you have continuing losses, it is a good time to return to simulated trading so that you can regain the feel for the market and reestablish your confidence in yourself and your judgment. A good rule of discipline is to revert to paper trading when you feel out of sync with the market. Take time out and reestablish your feel for the ebb and flow of the market. In which direction is the market moving? Listen to the music of the market and not the silence when the music has stopped.

As I stated above, I do not subscribe to purely mathematical guidelines. You should have a good, sensible, logical, and rational reason for entering into every trade. If your reasoning is correct, then you will make money. If your reasoning is wrong, then you should contain your loss. You want to trade based upon commonsense rationality and reason. You trade because you sense opportunity. Even though you are trading rationally, you may still lose money in an irrational market. The market does not always act in a logical and rational manner, and you must take it as a given that you can lose money because the market is choppy. A slump is not a reason to give up trading.

You should trade when it feels right and when you have a plan. You must have a plan for every order you want executed. The trading plan should encompass your fallback position if the market goes against you. You must know your position and your reaction to every price movement after you initiate a trading position. Never think that paper profits are *not* real just because you have not as yet realized those profits. Likewise, trading losses are not paper losses; they too are real—and painful.

NEVER TRADE WITH MONEY YOU CANNOT AFFORD TO LOSE

An old Wall Street adage states that you should never trade with scared money. If you can't afford to lose capital, you most probably will. The self-fulfilling prophecy will come true because your mind-set has a siege mentality, which is dedicating more of your energies to defensive trading than to aggressive trading.

You shouldn't risk the homestead on any single trade or investment. One of your brokerage firm's criteria in determining a person's suitability for DAET is the availability of trading capital. You shouldn't be trading unless you understand that your capital is subject to market price change (risk) with respect to every trade.

Traders do not trade for excitement or passion. They trade for profit. As a DAET trader, you should not be operating from white heat to white heat. Trading should not make you nervous or tense. Pumping adrenaline is not a positive sign. Successful traders, to the contrary, should be severely detached and unemotional. You want to have the ability to look at your own trading position and analyze what went right and what went wrong. If the market has not met your initial expectations, extricate yourself from the position efficiently.

Diversify your positions. Do not accumulate ever-augmenting positions in the same stock. The problem with accumulating an inventory is that when you have too many shares of an apparently good stock and are most vulnerable, the stock may turn against you, causing your profits to disappear. This is why you want to view trading as a moving express train on which you can detrain at the next profitable station.

EMOTIONAL FACTORS IN TRADING

Will you lose your lunch if you lose money on your first trade? I have closely observed new traders and have noticed how important the control of one's emotions becomes for successful trading. You can't take losses personally. Losses are not a personal affront to you. Even the best traders will have losing days. It is hard enough to control matters within your personal sphere of influence, such as losing weight on a diet. I once went on a diet for two weeks and all I lost was two weeks.

Ergo, if it is difficult to control what you eat, you know that it is impossible for you to control the market movements and to predict every trend correctly.

I have developed a list of a number of emotional factors that come into play and must be overcome (the physical ones are emotionally based):

Fear

A sense of information overload

A feeling of being overwhelmed

Shock at money loss

The Kenny Rogers syndrome—you have to know when to hold them, know when to fold them, know when to walk away, and know when to run.

Hormonal dump from the endocrine glands (the fight or flight syndrome)

Nausea

Loose bowels

Loss of consciousness

Every trader has experienced some emotional factors at one time or another. Debilitating emotions arise from a sense of helplessness when the market is turning against your established position and seconds turn into hours. You must learn to react appropriately when the market is running against you because, as noted above, you cannot control the market. You can only control yourself.

Some major league baseball batting champions hit only .333. This means that the champ is out of the game two times in every three at bats. Even though the very best baseball hitters are out twice as much as they get on base, they still command heavy salaries. A different percentage system carries over to trading where you should be right more than you are wrong based upon the trader's edge of having instant prices and instant access to the market. As long as the number and amount of your losses are kept under control, you can take small but tolerable losses. You will win by ending the bad trades quickly and riding the profitable trades as long as you dare.

Traders who follow my advice can have positive gain in the long run. In trading, you cannot expect to win 100 percent of the time. But good traders can expect to be right more than they are wrong. Your training and experience are the key to success and the yellow brick road to profitable trading.

LEARN FROM YOUR MISTAKES

Every successful trader has suffered losses and market rejection at one time or another. Failure and success are not two opposite ends of the spectrum because of the educational and self-improvement values of failure. Success is a path and not a goal. Trading errors do not constitute failure assuming that you learn from the mistakes. Truth will sooner come out of error than from confusion (Sir Francis Bacon). Trading success is a way of life in which each failure is one of the building blocks upon which success is based. Turn minor setbacks into positive learning experiences by determining what went wrong and experimenting until you find a trading style that works for you. When Thomas Edison was searching for the filament that would illuminate the electric light bulb, he suffered over 800 failures. When his helper complained about the wasted time, Edison replied that the time had not been wasted because they already found more than 800 alloys that did not work.

In order to calculate risk, you must have a great sense of timing. Rockefeller Center is a keystone office building in an exclusive neighborhood in New York City. Yet when it was built in the Great Depression of the 1930s, it was virtually untenanted. The Great Depression was raging and the unrented Rockefeller Center was a drag on the real estate market. The Rockefeller family had to use its great influence to move its own Standard Oil Company and the Chase Manhattan Bank into the building.

In order to achieve the biggest bang for you trading buck in the shortest time, you must be *time competent.* You must be able to gauge future prices based upon present situations. View the *now* in your life as a running summary of the past and the key to the future. Live in the present, but experience the market so that you are anticipating future market prices.

Intuition counts in decision making and risk taking. Traders don't quite know why, but their intuition tells them what to do. We say that they feel it in their "guts." Trading is sometimes a gut decision. Obviously, some traders are more intuitive than others.

DAET traders want to balance the mathematical probability of success with their special intuition when they decide whether to take a trading risk. To be more precise, traders should ride with the probabilities and with their intuition. When the probabilities of success are high and their intuition "feels" right, then traders should take the trading risk.

The best strategy to curtail risk is not to make any trading mistakes. But the only way to do that is not to trade—trading losses are part of the game. I can tell you that the next best strategy is to cut each trading loss as soon as the market turns adverse to your position.

It is OK to have a trading loss. It is not acceptable to allow that small trading loss to turn into a large trading mistake by watching that loss grow and not taking steps to close out that position and mitigate your loss. As they say in banking, there are bad loans and there are stupid loans. A stupid loan is an additional loan to the same person to whom the banker has already made a bad loan. As you already know, the most effective way not to lose money is to stop losses as quickly as practical. Don't allow losses to become blank checks.

Fear stops risk taking. Once you have learned the rules of risk taking, you will only take appropriate trading risks. Once you have learned how to analyze and benefit from your trading mistakes, you should have the power to overcome fear. Trading decisions are like all other decisions in life. Following the rules for trading should free you from the fear of failure, which haunts most individuals. Our major anxiety is a fear of failure and loss. Rid yourself of this free-floating uncertainty. In western society our culture applauds success. In eastern philosophies, the nobleness of defeat against overwhelming odds is epic. Don't be afraid of failing. The worst that can happen is that you start all over again with better ideas and greater experience.

> **There is no failure greater than not trying to succeed.**

NASDAQ INTERNATIONAL TRADING

Nasdaq trading has already become international to a limited extent. Nasdaq has a subsidiary called Nasdaq International Ltd., which is headquartered in London. Its mission is to support NASD members in London, serve as a liaison to international companies seeking to list securities on Nasdaq, encourage foreign institutional participation in Nasdaq stocks, and heighten the international image of the NASD and its markets.

Nasdaq also offers an international service that was designed to give Nasdaq an international cachet and worldwide flair. Nasdaq's international service was proposed as an extension to the Nasdaq stock market's trading systems to allow early morning trading from 3:30 a.m. to 9:00 a.m. Eastern Standard Time on each U.S. trading day. This Nasdaq service is designed to enable participants to monitor trades during London market hours. NASD members are eligible to participate in this session through their U.S. trading facilities or through those of an approved U.K. affiliate.

To date this service has proved to be a total economic bust. When the NASD inaugurated its international service, it flooded the news services with news releases and image advertising flaunting its newly acquired worldwide status. From that point forward, there has been almost no volume of international trade. In fact, almost every morning the Nasdaq system issues a short announcement to the effect that no international trades occurred during the previous night.

THE STOCK MARKET OF THE FUTURE

The past shows us the future. As Shakespeare wrote "What's past is prologue." The markets of the future will be computer accessible, transparent, and open to all. In the future, specialists on the major securities exchanges will lose their vested ability to monopolize the market in any particular stock and will be forced to computerize and display their internal book so that all market participants will have equal price disclosure of support and resistance levels.

All markets will be and should be interrelated. The occasional price dislocations that Direct Access Electronic Traders now use to profit from intermarket arbitrage should no longer exist because arbitrage is a product of inefficient markets. The core market is the theoretical and actual place where all orders will meet.

The advent of ECNs will prove to be the basis of real 24-hour-a-day trading that will be available worldwide. Eventually, ECNs will permit the display of orders from anyone, anytime, anywhere in the world. Because the mechanism for transparency will be absolute and access will be routine through a multitude of interconnected computer networks, there will no longer be a need to restrict market hours for the convenience of the market makers, the industry, and the regulators, and trading could occur as long as there were willing buyers and sellers. It may prove to be more convenient for most Americans to trade in the evening after they come home from a day's work. Instead of watching mindless sitcoms and other TV trash, many market participants would gainfully be spending their time in the market. I believe that a good market will draw a larger audience than a popular sporting event. After all, trading is a participatory sport rather than an idle spectator sport and a trader's potential injuries will be financial rather than physical.

The future of the market makers appears to be bleak and dismal. Many literate people will be trading through a personal computer. I foresee a financial Internet that is totally secure and operating in real time. Every stock, commodity, and futures contract will be listed in every trading market, and the computer program will be seeking the best price in the best market. All executions will be instantaneous with the push of a button. Few will use conventional brokers for execution of orders. Brokers usually don't know anything except what the firm's research and sales departments want them to sell in the first place. Brokers in the future will probably be financial guarantors of your trade because strangers will not want to trade with an unknown entity over a computer terminal. Your broker will furnish research analysis and information relating to price quotes, access to the market, and automatic order execution. In fact, tomorrow looks exactly like DAET does today. Brokerage houses will exist to provide tax information in form and substance acceptable to the IRS.

Electronic markets are now international and worldwide. A proper DAET system can reach anywhere in the world a phone can reach. The next stage will be fewer and faster remote routers on a private business Internet so that anyone in the world can trade on any market as expeditiously as locals. Non-English-speaking people may have English language problems, but they can certainly understand the international language of numbers.

According to at least one professor, those same SEC Order Handling Rules that created the ECNs would also allow for decimal pricing. Decimal pricing is pricing in pennies. Any investor or DAET trader would much prefer decimal pricing to sub-eighth increments. Let's face it. The stock market is one of the few major markets artificially priced in sub-eighths (such as thirty-seconds, sixteenths, eighths, or quarters of a dollar). Fractional sub-eighth pricing is unnatural in the United States. Our economy doesn't normally tolerate prices expressed in fractions rather than in decimals. You would be dumbfounded if every item in the supermarket was priced in sub-quarter-of-a-dollar price gradations. Passing price changes to the customer highlights the problem. When your food store raises the price of milk, it increases the price in pennies and not by a quarter or an eighth of a dollar. Consumers would have a devil of a time with unwieldy and miscellaneous fractions.

For years, I have been an advocate of decimal pricing. Recently, the regulators and the industry have agreed to permit decimal pricing as quickly as possible. Of course, they had to. Many stock exchanges like the Toronto Exchange were already trading in decimal prices. Interestingly enough, the empirical evidence proved that Nasdaq stocks, which were cross-traded on the Toronto Exchange in decimals, were cheaper in Canada than they were in the U.S. markets. Decimal pricing on Nasdaq and the exchanges will reduce the risk of overcoming the spread to DAET traders. Traders have to beat the spread in order to make a profit. It helps if the spread is in pennies instead of higher fractions of a dollar. Traders and investors are buying the underlying volatility of a stock and want to pay as little as possible for the spread.

RULES FOR SUCCESS

Go home *flat, no worries.*

Learn to cut losses.

Ride your profits.

Position yourself to profit on downward movements of securities.

Always treat trading as a business.

Learn to profitably trade all markets.

Control your ego.

Have fun!

WAYS TO LOSE MONEY

Hold overnight positions.

Trade into too wide of a spread.

Enter too late.

Exit too late.

Chase a stock.

Take a stock with too narrow of a trading range.

Play with scared money.

Speculate on hearsay.

Trade on the news.

Trade stocks with low volume.

Become distracted or unfocused and let a stock get away from you.

Keep too many positions open to keep track of them all.

Think you know more than the market.

Trade to get even because you had a fight with your significant other.

Trade when you shouldn't.

Don't cut losses.

DEEP DARK SECRETS OF THE SOES BANDIT

I AM THE MAN WHO ROCKED WALL STREET

As SEC Chairman Arthur Levitt, the architect of the new enlightened regulatory environment, proclaimed with appropriate statesmanship:

> Markets exist by the grace of investors. When those who direct them lose sight of that cardinal rule, and sacrifice investor interests on the altar of short-term gain, then far from helping their market, they hurt it. History regularly attests to this truth: witness the New York Stock Exchange in the 1930s, the American Stock Exchange in the 1960s, and now Nasdaq in the 1990s.

Although never intending to do so, I became a revolutionary who dared to try to change the market's cheating heart and the Aladdin who freed the genie of DAET for the masses. I don't mean to blow my own horn, but I was one of the very people from the industry who dared to fight what seemed to be insurmountable odds so that anyone could participate electronically in the market. I was helped by Linda Lerner, Esq., our general counsel. I was fighting the established entrenched tradition, the market makers, the NASD, other regulators, the best lawyers money could buy, and biased press coverage that only millions of advertising dollars could buy.

The story begins in 1963 when Congress identified a number of anticompetitive and manipulative practices in the securities markets. The 1963 Special Study of the Securities Markets identified the following problems:

Failure to honor quotations

Trading ahead of customers

Hand holding

Friendliness among traders ranging from sharing customer trade information to secretly investing in joint accounts

Blackballing

Nontransparent pricing

Wide spreads

The Special Study concluded that "competition in these markets may at times be impaired resulting in an appearance of competition that may not always accord with reality."

To further address these issues, in 1975 Congress mandated change to a national market system with initiatives designed to:

Create greater transparency

Foster greater reliability for OTC quotations

Consolidate and disseminate marketwide quotes

Secure firm quote obligations

More than 30 years after Congress's initial vision, virtually nothing had changed. Once again, in 1994, history repeated itself when the SEC and the Department of Justice initiated formal inquiries into Nasdaq trading and the leading market makers for substantially the same abuses that had rocked the foundations of the stock market in 1963. Old trading abuses were integrated into the new trading technology and were manipulated to allow the continued cheating of the investing public.

A subtle, but extremely effective, conspiracy evolved over the years in which all too many people associated with the Nasdaq stock market participated or acquiesced in illegal, immoral, and unethical activities, whether knowingly or not, including certain regulators whether conscientiously or not. There were *no* whistle-blowers except for one official, who tried to make a difference but was hushed up.

All the supposedly competing market makers found it easier to cooperate with each other and systemically create a very noncompetitive "competitive" market which set up the opportunity for them to extract excessively wide spreads from their customers. The old-time Teddy Roosevelt, Thomas E. Dewey, consumer-friendly, antibusiness, stiff regulatory attitude, with staunch trust-busting religion, had been swapped by the *old regulators* at the NASD for a policy of market-maker accommodation. As SEC Chairman Arthur Levitt regretfully commented about a defeated, discredited, and shamed NASD:

> Nor has the SEC emerged unscathed. To the extent these
> practices took place on our watch, we should have acted
> sooner. We, as well as the NASD, need to be faster and more
> vigilant. To assure that the public interest is protected.

The nature of the shakedown reads like a financial caper novel. The principal plan was artificially to establish and then synthetically maintain superwide spreads between the quoted bid and ask price on Nasdaq. The exorbitant spread enabled the market makers to increase their profits on both the buy and the sell side of the transaction, with more than enough money left over to pay for order flow to compliant referring brokers.

Chairman Levitt best summarized the conspiracy, on August 8, 1996, when announcing the settlement of an SEC enforcement action against the NASD after an 18-month investigation:

> I will state it simply and up front. We have found a widespread
> course of conduct among market makers to coordinate their
> quotes. Investors paid too much and received too little, when
> they bought and sold their stock on Nasdaq. New traders were,
> as a matter of course, trained in this fashion. Over time, this
> practice became the expected standard. In some instances,

those who did not comply were harassed and penalized, even if
they had acted in the best interests of investors. . . .

Nor was the pricing convention the only unacceptable practice.
The NASD failed to ensure the accuracy and fairness of quotation and transaction information—the backbone of securities
trading. It failed to apply certain rules to its members, and
selectively enforced rules against others. The NASD allowed
the interests of large market making firms to have undue
influence over the conduct of its affairs and the regulation of
its market.

The evidence—gathered from hundreds of witnesses, thousands
of hours of tapes, and more than a million pages of documents—shows that the NASD did not fulfill its most basic
responsibilities—and I quote from its charter: to promote just
and equitable principles of trade for the protection of investors.
On the contrary, American investors were hurt—large and
small, sophisticated and inexperienced, institutional and individual—all were hurt by these practices.

THE SEC CONSENT DECREE AGAINST
THE NASD

The most awesome and dramatic event since my last book has
been the SEC consent agreement with the NASD. On August
8, 1996, the U.S. Securities and Exchange Commission
released its findings that the NASD failed to enforce compliance with its own rules and the federal securities laws. The
SEC simultaneously announced the institution of an administrative enforcement proceeding and the NASD's consent to
the entry of an order censuring the NASD. The findings were
set forth in an *SEC Report of Investigation* regarding the
NASD and the Nasdaq market.

The SEC broke up a tacit conspiracy that artificially maintained excessive spreads between the bid and ask price on
Nasdaq. The evidence was monolithic without fracture in its
portrayal of broad-based market-maker collusion to rig prices
and eliminate competition. Certain key officials at the NASD

disappeared and then resurfaced in providential jobs with the collusive market makers.

A volcano of SEC wrath erupted against the NASD. Essentially, the SEC came to require empirical evidence from the NASD correlating proposed rule changes to real results. No longer did the market-maker-dominated NASD wear white hats and continue to be the perennial good guys like the heroes in old black-and-white movies of the wild west. A barrage of criticism from academia, the media, and me was the prelude to the SEC and Department of Justice investigation into the conduct and affairs of the NASD and many powerful market-making firms.

The industry had speculated that the SEC and the Department of Justice inquiries would be harmless; these thoughts evaporated quickly as the U.S. Department of Justice all but indicted the NASD and 24 leading market makers. Even though criminal indictments were eliminated as a possibility fairly early in the Department of Justice investigation, market-maker smugness melted into concern as the SEC changed the rules of the game and in fact spelled out the potential demise of the "good old boy" network.

The NASD and the major market makers entered into a proposed consent judgment in federal court under which *future* violations of the consent decree will be cause for criminal actions. The NASD was allowed to maintain its claim of innocence by not contesting the charges. Instead of jailing the NASD officials (who permitted an environment fraught with abuse and cast a blind eye to fairness and morality), the SEC enacted encompassing changes to the NASD structure and to the trading rules. This seemed to be the only rational action. Otherwise public confidence in the entire market structure would have disappeared and could have caused a major meltdown. I would like to think that any future violations of the consent agreement would cause the market makers to be treated under the one-bite doggy rule where vicious dogs have to put down on the second bite.

The SEC's investigation found that the Nasdaq market did not consistently operate in an open and freely competitive manner. Furthermore, Nasdaq market makers engaged in a variety of abusive practices to suppress competition and mislead investors. As the primary regulator of the Nasdaq market, the NASD *failed* to carry out is obligations to oversee the market and the conduct of its market makers. It was the age-old corruption question of who regulates the regulators?

This wholesale-retail differential, or spread, exists in all businesses and is acceptable when true price competition exists, because you can obtain different prices from competing dealers. The market makers crawled over that thin line toward ostensible criminal activity when all the wholesalers and the retailers conspired to maintain wide spreads and discouraged anyone else from trading at competitive prices. Price fixing is essentially a rejection of the free-market forces that drive business. Rather than allowing competition to set prices for products and services, price fixing creates a fictitious marketplace. As a result, consumers or investors pay what the conspirators misrepresent the market price to be, rather than the real market price.

Nasdaq market makers stood in virtual lockstep, marching to an anticompetitive pricing "convention" in which many securities were quoted *only* in even eighths (i.e., $\frac{1}{4}$, $\frac{1}{2}$, $\frac{3}{4}$, and 1). As a result, these securities were quoted with minimum inside spreads of $\frac{1}{4}$, thereby increasing the transaction costs paid by many investors when buying or selling those stocks. Nasdaq stocks were rarely traded at odd eighths (i.e., $\frac{1}{8}$, $\frac{3}{8}$, $\frac{5}{8}$, and $\frac{7}{8}$), while the same stocks were traded at odd eighths or better when market makers traded among themselves on Instinet and other private trading systems. In effect, there were prices quoted for the public and *real* prices disseminated only on private trading venues for professionals and not available to John Q. Public. As we have discussed throughout this book, Direct Access Electronic Trading puts the real prices in the hands of everyone so that you can participate on a level playing field. Needless to say, this is good for you and bad for market makers. The NASD allowed one of my companies, Domestic Securities, Inc., to be a market maker in 50 stocks. I decided to cross the line by quoting my prices in odd-eighth-point increments. Talk about innovative thinking. My quoted prices were an eighth of a point better than the competition. At Domestic Securities we took pride in cutting the spreads in order to foster competition. Yet orders did not come rolling in—but the spreads did decrease. When I broke the line by making a market at the odd-eighth price, I was excoriated by the market makers (for allowing the free market to establish the price of Nasdaq stocks).

This so-called "pricing convention" (a fancy name invented by the colluders for price fixing) was generally put forth by market makers as a work ethic, a time-honored tradition or professional norm that other market makers were expected to follow. The pricing convention was sometimes enforced through intimidation and actual infliction of financial harm.

Most interestingly, and not unexpectedly, the NASD failed to investigate allegations of price fixing and other market-maker improprieties even though the NASD had been made aware of these practices since 1990 by one of its own executives. It always amazes me that doctors, teachers, and neighbors never notice signs of child abuse until after the child dies from neglect. As far as the NASD regulators were concerned, all seemed to be under control at the market makers' trading departments.

The SEC investigation also found that the NASD's surveillance and enforcement of important market integrity rules was inadequate and that the NASD failed to vigorously enforce rules applicable to its market makers. Numerous market makers failed to honor their quotations and repeatedly failed to report their trades on time, as required by SEC and NASD rules. Certain market makers also refused to honor their trades in a discriminatory fashion against disfavored market participants such as options traders, competing specialists, short sellers, and SOES order entry firms.

One of the major benefits of the investigations was that the real bandits were unmasked. The term *SOES bandit* is now an anachronism and a joke. The new respectability and credibility became the threshold to go forward with Direct Access Electronic Trading.

To put this all-encompassing conspiracy in perspective, one-eighth of a point does not sound like a great amount of money. It adds $125 on to the purchase price of 1000 shares. If you were mugged in the street for $125, you would probably be screaming bloody murder. But when robbery happens as a matter of routine during a commonplace business transaction, you don't complain because it is business as usual and you are conditioned to expect it. And there is no one to complain to who would be sympathetic to your plight.

Most major stocks used to move in quarters and seldom in eighths of a point. Could it be that no market maker or trader ever considered the possibility of moving stock prices by only eighth of a point to create a little real competition based upon price? I was astonished that virtually no market maker or trader ever broke the line. The reason, of course, was that the industry wanted to keep spreads artificially wide. The industry maintained high spreads by collusive agreement in which no one would change a bid from a quarter to an eighth of a point.

The SEC censured the NASD for running a stock market that was akin to Dodge City with no sheriff. The SEC ordered the NASD to clean up its act and run a fair market. For years, I condemned the NASD for closing its eyes and turning a deaf ear to the complaints of the general public.

The SEC imposed significant remedial measures on the NASD. These "remedial" steps appeared "punitive" because they related to the NASD governance and regulatory structure. Other SEC-ordered changes included the introduction of new Order Handling Rules, declared effective in January 1997.

REGULATORY ACCOMMODATION

It appears as if the SEC and the NASD have entered into a separation agreement pending a final divorce. The NASD has sincerely earned the indignation of the SEC and brought the ire of real regulation upon itself. At this point it is no longer politically correct to be too closely associated with the market-making community. The activities of the market makers and their methods of dealing with the investing public have been the subject of exposés in major financial publications. Even so, the NASD will surely continue to advance proposals to the SEC on behalf of its members for advantages friendly to the financial community and taxing to the general investing public, including traders. However, it seems likely that the SEC will only approve regulatory changes that benefit the public.

This is not to say that a different execution system will not eventually replace SOES as a trading mechanism, but you can rest assured that DAET is here to stay. If you just look at the actions of the SEC, you can see for yourself that any proposed trading system that impedes public access and the flow of information will not pass muster. The new reality is that the SEC will not rubber-stamp any NASD proposal that curtails investor access to the best market or limits the flow of market knowledge to the investing public.

If you want to predict the future, look at what people do instead of what they say. Examine what the NASD is proposing but do not rely upon it as gospel. Really focus on what Mr. Levitt and the new, enlightened SEC are actually doing. I cannot remember a time when there has been more positive leadership over the integrity of markets. Mr. Levitt was the former president of the AMEX and has extensive background in business and with the Wall Street community. Mr. Levitt seems to be more investor oriented than his predecessors and appears to be unwilling to accept NASD rule proposals at face value without supporting empirical data.

The SEC is now executing the mandate Congress issued in 1975 to make all markets transparent so that all participants can benefit from best-price information in the core market. The regulators are no longer as accommodative to the NASD and its members as they used to be. The national regulators are changing the market mechanism so that true competition by price and order size will prevail. In my judgment, the regulatory future will be much friendlier for average investors and DAET traders largely because the impediments to successful trading have diminished. Many advantages previously enjoyed by the market makers and the industry insiders have been removed.

To paraphrase the late Eldridge Cleaver, the Black Panther leader, "You are either the problem or the solution." It seems that the SEC now knows that the market makers were the problem and the transparency of markets was the solution. The future of Direct Access Electronic Trading is now more secure. The environment for DAET will improve because the regulators will not reverse direction and return control of market regulation to anyone incapable of honoring the public trust. The SEC has forced the NASD (in lieu of a financial penalty) to commit to spend an aggregate of $100 million over 5 years to enhance enforcement, surveillance, and compliance with Nasdaq trading rules. In addition, the NASD was also ordered to:

Adopt a rule explicitly prohibiting improper market-maker coordination

Design and implement a state-of-the-art order audit trail to provide for better surveillance of trading rules

Improve surveillance and enforcement of trade reporting violations

Improve surveillance and enforcement of laws against backing-away violations, including the establishment of a complaint center to respond immediately to backing-away complaints

Improve the surveillance and examination of order handling to ensure that customer orders are executed appropriately

Establish objective membership admission standards

Provide for greater involvement by representatives of the public and other NASD constituencies on the NASD's boards and policy committees

Insulate the NASD staff from the commercial interests of NASD members

Establish an effective, independent internal audit office reporting solely to the NASD's board of governors

Establish professional hearing officers for disciplinary hearings

Retain an independent consultant to report to the board of governors and the Commission on Compliance with respect to all of the above undertakings

The NASD proposed to operate through two subsidiaries. The market activity was separated from a new regulatory organization. NASD Regulation (NASDR), Inc., now has primary responsibility for regulatory matters. The other subsidiary, the Nasdaq Stock Market, has primary responsibility for operating the Nasdaq stock market.

The SEC, having determined that the NASD failed in its self-regulatory duties, "remedially" reorganized the NASD board to include a majority of nonindustry members. The hope is that these outside directors will follow their own independent hearts and minds and lead the NASD in a fashion congruent with their own sense of fairness and integrity.

How do nonindustry members become elected to the board if the members of the nominating committee are the same people previously in charge of the NASD? While all board members are created equal, I pray that the industry board members are not more equal. The NASD swears that members of all three of these boards were *carefully* selected to represent a wide range of the NASD's constituencies. I have a friend who is such a doubter that his colleagues made a baseball cap for him containing the words "We'll See" on the peak.

The NASD swears that it will not unduly influence its committee and business office system, which in the past anonymously wielded the executioner's ax of bad news toward DAET firms. This concept of balance, of industry and outside, or in some cases, a majority of nonindustry members, will allegedly be extended to certain important committees of the NASD and its subsidiaries. These include the NASD Audit Committee, the NASDR Executive Committee, the NASDR National Business Conduct Committee, the NASDR National Arbitration and Mediation Committee, the Nasdaq Executive Committee, and the Nasdaq Quality of Markets Committee. It was no accident, I believe, that no DAET firm had ever been represented on a committee at this critical juncture. These steps, if performed with integrity, represent significant changes in the NASD's self-regulatory process.

More NASD affirmative action includes a 7 percent increase in NASDR staff for enforcement, examination, and market regulation programs. NASDR has initiated measures to enhance the enforcement of the trade reporting, firm quote, customer limit order handling, and other market-making rules, and has begun the development of an enhanced audit trail. The NASDR has also changed its disciplinary processes to include hearing officers and added procedures aimed at achieving greater efficiency and fairness. The NASD still doesn't have a bill of rights, but the revolution is still in its infancy.

The NASD also promised to enhance its systems for trading and market surveillance, including compliance with late trade reporting and various other NASD trading rules. The NASD has created two new offices, the Office of Individual Investor Services and the Office of the Ombudsman, *to more fully serve* the interest of investors and other NASD constituents.

The board of governors of the NASD and the board of directors of the NASDR have authorized $25 million and have committed to expend an additional $75 million over the next 5 years to enhance its legacy computer systems. Of course, the NASD giveth and the NASD taketh away, because the respective boards reserve the right to renegotiate with the SEC if the $100 million expenditure is not achievable or feasible. The world will be watching to see if "renege" is the only part of renegotiate that the NASD implements. Remember that you heard it from me first.

As discussed above, the SEC's new Order Handling Rules became effective on January 20, 1997. The Order Handling Rules represented constructive change for the better and ushered sweeping changes in the operations and accountability of the brokerage industry and heralded the new frontier of trading. Most significantly, there is nothing in the SEC's view which limits the new Order Handling Rules only to Nasdaq, and they aren't. There is no logical reason why the specialist should be necessary for the purported auction sale of securities on the New York Stock Exchange. The computerized technology of today has already eliminated most of the specialist's function.

NASDAQ IS FLAWED IN CONCEPT

Nasdaq is a negotiated market where hundreds of millions of shares trade each day, and Nasdaq wants to run the market like in days of old when only a million shares a day traded. Nasdaq was historically the market for smaller issues of newer, thinly traded stocks. The over-the-counter market was a negotiated market. Today, Nasdaq volume is even higher than the NYSE trading volume. Nasdaq's old advertising promoted Nasdaq—the "market for the next one hundred years." The enhanced volume has shifted the whole concept of Nasdaq from a negotiated market to a something else. A conceptual distortion arises. The question is whether Nasdaq can continue to be a negotiated market or must change to a more auction-oriented order-driven market? The stated belief of the NASD is that market makers should interact with all orders in a dealer-quote-based market as opposed to an auction-based market like the NYSE where buyer meets seller in a public and open forum. In an auction market, buyer meets seller without the need for an intermediary. A specialist on the NYSE only interacts in order to prevent unnecessary price volatility when there is no buyer or seller from the public.

Highly capitalized, widely traded stocks like Intel, Microsoft, and CISCO appear not to require a negotiated market. The dealer market of the past does not serve the investing or trading needs of the public today. Nasdaq wants to be the market of the future, but it wants to run it with the "pink sheet" mentality it used to run the market with 30 years ago.

The nature and the quality of many stocks trading on Nasdaq have changed. Nasdaq can no longer be a private resort. When you are expanding your business, you can't be a small boutique at the same time that you want to be a mass distributor. For Nasdaq to maintain a dealer-based negotiated mentality and still claim to be the high-tech market for the twenty-first century is inconsistent. Nasdaq will have to alter its market to accommodate the realities of the new electronic environment, and the SEC has already taken steps to take the market in that direction.

Prior to 1996, when the SEC caused major changes to be implemented, the NASD served three mutually conflicting and diametrically opposed functions. I call this functional trinity the Three Hats of the NASD. They are:

1. SRO responsibilities
2. Membership organization
3. Nasdaq market operations

SRO Responsibilities

First, the NASD is supposed to be the public watchdog over its member firms. The NASD is a self-regulatory organization (SRO) authorized by Congress to supervise, and regulate all the activities of its broker-dealer members. The NASD acts as a police officer and watchdog. The NASD also has authority to propose rules and to interpret the rules it has proposed for the SEC's approval (an approval that was often all too readily delivered based upon historic relationships). NASD officials carried with them the color of right, and their proposals were seldom challenged by the SEC's Market Regulation Division. This arrangement gave the NASD officials excessive power to grant the wishes of their influential members, who often sat on the major committees and the board of governors.

Membership Organization

Second, the NASD is a dues-paying membership organization. As such, it looks to advance the interests of its members.

Unfortunately, advancing the interest of its members many times flies in the face of protecting the public.

NASDAQ MARKET OPERATIONS

Last, the NASD operates the Nasdaq market, which is a major entrepreneurial phenomenon seeking to be the "market for the next one hundred years." Thus, the NASD had a conflict of interest in the way it should have run Nasdaq. For example, was Nasdaq run in a way that deliberately permitted the abuses found by the Department of Justice and the SEC? Should the NASD have allowed Nasdaq to become the plaything of its market-making members? Some could say that the NASD slanted Nasdaq regulations for the benefit of its powerful market-making constituency at the expense of the public and to the detriment of its electronic order entry firm members. Others intimate that the NASD officials should have used their gatekeeper authority in a more just and equitable fashion. Many of these NASD officials have since retired or found alternative positions, but a few still remain.

As part of the NASD's procedures, all disputes between members and the NASD itself are adjudicated in proceedings run by the NASD. In effect, the NASD is the police, accuser, judge, and jury when it decides to take an action against a member. One might call the adjudication structure unfair. I, for one, am doing so. Appearance before a disciplinary committee used to be all too serious, but also senseless because the hearing officers were often your competition—and in the case of electronic trading they were your worst enemies. They would never even think of excusing themselves from their position of power; this was exactly the position they wanted to be in because there was no downside to them for the outcomes they ordered.

CLASS-ACTION UPDATE

The SEC consent agreement was like throwing soft rocks at the NASD, because no public fines were levied against the wrongdoers and no one at the NASD or any market-making firm was ushered from the office in handcuffs or even immediately discharged. There was no cry of outrage after the consent agreement.

During the SEC investigation, a number of private cases were filed against the major market makers for civil damages. All the individual actions were certified as a class-action lawsuit and consolidated in the U.S. District Court for the Southern District of New York in New York City. U.S. District Court Judge Robert Sweet granted class-action status against 33 Nasdaq market makers for allegedly fixing stock prices. In a 94-page decision, Judge Sweet amalgamated all of the complaints into one megacase.

The class included investors who made trades through the major market makers from May 1, 1989, to May 24, 1994, and the class eventually could total about 6.3 million people and institutions. The 33 defendants, which included many of Wall Street's largest firms, like Goldman Sachs & Co.; Merrill Lynch & Co.; CS First Boston Corp.; and Donaldson, Lufkin & Jenrette Securities, Inc., had argued that the 33 cases should not be granted class-action status because the individual suits didn't address common questions. The class had invested in 1,659 Nasdaq securities with different brokerage firms at various times.

The suit accused the major market makers of conspiring to manipulate spreads between bid and ask prices on Nasdaq securities. Not surprisingly, the dealers were accused of rigging the prices in order to maximize their profits.

The class actions were based upon the existence of an unlawful conspiracy to eliminate odd-eighth quotations in order to increase price spreads in violation of the U.S. antitrust laws. The publication of econometric data indicating apparent market-maker price fixing was the catalyst for the class-action lawsuits. The lawsuits were driven by more than a million pages of documents in the Department of Justice probe and by very credible academic studies documenting the allegations by reputable professors at well-known universities. The NASD appeared to be shaken by the publicity surrounding the 1994 report of Professors Paul H. Shultz and William G. Christie entitled "Why Do NASDAQ Market Makers Avoid Odd-Eighth Quotes?" The market makers even held a mass meeting at Bear Stearns in order to come to one another's defense.

The class-action cases should have been great sport because of the solidity of the evidence. My prediction had been that the only hard-dollar reimbursement for the victims of the fraud would come from the class-action awards. As of the writing of this book, the Wall Street securities firms have proposed to settle the class-action claims for over $1 *billion,* which sounds like a great deal of money until you put the dollars into perspective and realize that $1 billion is about one quarter's earnings for only one of the major market makers.

The settlement pain won't be evenly shared. In reaching the class-action settlement, the market makers used a pro rata formula under which each firm's contribution was based upon its share of Nasdaq trading. Under the settlement, the firms will still *officially* deny any wrongdoing. The market makers still won't admit that they did anything wrong. The market makers believed that their agreed-upon "convention" of pricing stocks in even eighths was honestly furthering the American spirit of capitalism. They even had the audacity to brand SOES traders as "bandits!" I believe that no one involved in the market during this period can ever again earn the public trust.

Merrill Lynch, the largest U.S. brokerage firm, will pay the most (about $100 million). The San Francisco–based Hambrecht & Quist Group was stuck with a proportionately large chunk of the settlement (about $20 million), because it was more dependent on trading Nasdaq stocks. The settlement is not a big deal even for Hambrecht in that $20 million will amount to about 75 cents a share to a company that First Call Corp. estimated will earn $1.90 for fiscal 1998.

However, the payout of $1 billion in and of itself demonstrates the genuine fear that the wrongdoers had of the huge potential liability. Certainly, $1 billion qualifies as much more than a chump-change nuisance value settlement when the interest alone (about $8 million a year) would have more than funded the legal fees until the year 3000. No member of the jury would have identified with the industry. The investors' attorneys would have earned their fees because the industry would have run them a merry chase through hills of paper and mountains of denial until the jury made justice with its ultimate verdict against the market makers and had assessed huge punitive damages for the manner in which the market makers treated the investing public. The settlement only looks bad for the market makers' current earnings report cards and current balance sheet.

Another real issue is the impact the settlement will have on investor confidence and on the Nasdaq market. Many market makers have been cutting back to adjust for falling profits. Merrill has already slashed the number of stocks in which it made a market from 850 to 450 and cut nine traders from its overhead.

The settlement confirmed everything I had been preaching. The average investor who completes and files onerous proof-of-loss forms with supporting documentation will be lucky if he or she nets enough for a Value Meal at McDonald's.

When the market makers settled the civil class actions for over a billion dollars, the story was reported in the last section of the *Wall Street Journal* and decently buried away where only the most interested of readers could find it. And it was released on Christmas Eve to be reported on the Friday after Christmas when anyone who counted was already on holiday.

NASDAQ PRICE RIGGING APPEARS TO CONTINUE

One recent study has indicated that the market-maker conspiracy to fix prices has continued. I am beginning to believe that the market makers are slow to learn from their past mistakes. According to a study released by the Electronic Traders Association (ETA), Nasdaq market makers have continued to maintain spreads by a new pricing convention. Most market makers are systemically posting their quotes in even sixteenths (two-sixteenths, four-sixteenths, etc.) rather than odd sixteenths (one-sixteenth, three-sixteenths, etc.). This has the effect of maintaining artificially wide bid/ask spreads (eighths rather than sixteenths). Pricing in one-sixteenth increments took effect in Nasdaq on June 2, 1997, for the purpose of facilitating narrower quoted spreads and enhancing competition.

These findings were contained in an ETA-commissioned study, "The Quotation Behavior of ECNs and Nasdaq Market Makers," conducted by Drs. Yusif Simaan (Associate Professor of Finance, Fordham University) and David K. Whitcomb (Professor of Finance at the Graduate School of Management of Rutgers University and President/CEO of Automated Trading Desk, Inc.). Covering the periods September 15–26 and October 20–31, 1997, the study examined, among other issues, the degree to which market makers attempt to avoid quote price competition in making Nasdaq markets. This practice of avoiding odd-increment quote prices identified by the Simaan-Whitcomb research is similar to the now famous Christie-Schultz finding in 1994 that market makers appeared to be engaging in tacit collusion by avoiding odd-eighth quotes. That paper led directly to the Department of Justice antitrust investigation, a class-action suit, an SEC censure of NASD, and the precedent-setting SEC Order Handling Rules, which were intended to restore price competition to the Nasdaq market.

Specifically, the Simaan-Whitcomb study found that the 10 major market makers posted their quotes in even sixteenths 93 percent of the time (with one market maker engaging in the practice 98 percent of the time). Even when a market maker was alone at the inside price (presumably the most competitive position), even sixteenths were posted 88 percent of the time. This compared poorly with "alone inside" orders posted on ECNs, which were found to be evenly distributed between odd sixteenths 49.7 percent of the time and even sixteenths 50.3 percent of the time.

The study also found that 9 out of the 10 market makers increased their frequency of posting odd-sixteenth quotes toward the end of the day. This was ostensibly because market makers, like electronic day traders, wish to lay off their inventory positions before the market closes and are forced to become more competitive in their quotation behavior. In a press release, Professor Whitcomb analyzed:

> This also explains why we see 50% odd-sixteenths on ECNs. Much of the trading there is market makers laying off their positions. When market makers have to trade in a competitive market trade anonymously with other market makers watching them, they behave competitively.

Professor Whitcomb added that the central finding of the ETA study was that there are two Nasdaq markets—an uncompetitive "advertised quote" market where retail investors are forced to trade and a fiercely competitive ECN market where many market makers anonymously trade.

The class-action settlement of over $1 billion was just a dime in a panhandler's cup when compared with market-maker profits. After a Department of Justice and SEC investigation, the entry of a federal court consent agreement never again to fix quoted spreads, and a class-action settlement, the market makers appear to have resumed the same anti-competitive behavior by reducing the "price convention" to a spread of an eighth instead of a quarter. It is the same thing all over again.

PAYMENT FOR ORDER FLOW

Payment for order flow is a practice whereby your broker receives a payment from the contra side of the transactions being executed for you. Remember that all transactions have two sides. For example, if you are buying a security, someone is selling it to you; and conversely, if you are selling a security, someone is buying it from you. Payment for order flow is akin to a kickback paid to your broker by the party representing the opposite side of your trade. Your broker pockets the referral amount, usually unbeknown to you because the disclosure is couched in vague language in the fine print on the flip side of your confirmation. This practice creates conflicts of interest that are mind-boggling in their impact.

Regrettably, payment for order flow has become the basis for the existence of the deep discount brokerage industry. In most cases the only reason the low commissions charged by deep discount brokers are possible is because the brokers are receiving payments for order flow that in many cases exceed by far the commission they are charging you. You may ask how is the payer of the payment for order flow able to make these payments to your broker (which amount to perhaps hundreds of millions annually) and at the same time deliver to you the best possible price to which you are entitled? *Your broker can't!*

Payers of order flow systematically maximize their profits by working against your orders, shaving fractions, and holding back fills to suit their objectives. What the market makers call the national best bid and offer, DAET traders call the worst legally acceptable price your broker can force you to accept. Your broker may have been able to find better execution prices but had no incentive to find them for you, despite the fact that the broker's fiduciary duty is to work in your best interest. After all, your broker didn't want to suffer the economic double whammy of relinquishing the 2 or 3 cents a share received from payment for order flow and possibly spending a 1 or 2 cents a share extra to get you the better price on one of the automated systems. DAET traders know what the real prices are and the correct execution price for their orders. A DAET trader could never tolerate being abused under a payment for order flow mechanism.

For whom is your broker really working, you who are paying from zero to $29.95 a trade or the market maker who is flowing back perhaps millions of dollars monthly? You don't have to be a genius to figure where you finish in this two-horse race. The paying market maker could trade with your broker hundreds of times a day while you trade with your broker only several times a year. Which will your brokerage firm favor in disputes? Which will it look to protect and which will it choose to favor, especially when you don't know for sure the real price you should have paid for the stock? All you are told is that your order was executed at some seemingly unpleasing "market" price.

It has been my experience that most people are often unhappily surprised when they get an execution back from their brokers. When they are selling, they seem to receive the bottom price; and when they are buying, they all too often seem to pay a price too high. I contend that this is not just a coincidence. All too often market makers are allowed to play with your orders for their benefit rather than being held to strict standards of business accountability.

It is totally illogical to me that payment for order flow is allowed to exist in today's politically correct world. Common sense says that a broker cannot represent both the buyer and the seller in the same transaction without a conflict of interest. Payment of order flow without a doubt compromises the integrity of the firm accepting it.

When E*Trade went public, it disclosed in its prospectus, dated August 16, 1996, exactly how material the receipt of payment for order flow was to its business.

> The Company has arrangements with various Nasdaq market makers, third market firms and exchanges to receive cash payments for order flow for routing trade orders to those firms for execution. The practice of receiving payments for order flow is widespread in the securities industry. Under applicable SEC regulations, receipt of these payments requires disclosure of such payments by the Company to its customers. The revenues received by the Company under these arrangements for the year ended September 30, 1995 and the nine months ended June 30, 1996 amounted to 20% and 22% of total revenues, respectively.

Remember that this is a percentage of revenue and not just profitability. How many businesses could survive today if their revenues decreased by over 20 percent with no offsetting reduction in costs. As a matter of fact, their cost might even be higher if the discount firm had to hire additional staff to search the market for the real best price. My experience indicates that the above percentages for payment for order flow are not unusual. In many other discount brokerage firms, revenues received from payment for order flow may even exceed this 22 percent amount.

Payment for order flow was an embarrassment for the now well-informed SEC. On the one hand, the new SEC would probably like to see payment for order flow go away. On the other hand, it is difficult to eliminate a policy that the old SEC had been condoning and has flourished for so long as to have entered the molecular structure of the market. Payment for order flow is so ingrained in the market system that its sudden elimination could be very disruptive to the market structure. The SEC may believe that its new Order Handling Rules will cure the blight of payment for order flow. Although the original concept of an eighth-of-a-point minimum spread did not solve the problems, the sub-eighth pricing (sixteenths and thirty-seconds) is doing the job far sooner than even I anticipated. Decimal pricing in pennies is on the immediate horizon. These dramatically reduced spreads will be so thin that market-maker profit margins will be squeezed to the point where the economics of payment for order flow will surely spell its demise or at least reduce it to where it may become inconsequential. Market makers are already facing reduced profit margins and in several cases have ceased to pay for order flow on limit orders.

The SEC's reasoning was to free the market so that the public would enforce its own economic self-interest by placing thousands of limit orders in between the spreads, thereby creating a truly tight spread and highly liquid order-driven market—a new market that would no longer be able to support large payments for order flow, thus legitimizing the market without any significant structural disruptions. This was a plan so well conceived that I wish I could take credit for it.

A recent article from the *Wall Street Journal* reported that market makers are reducing the number of stocks in which they make markets because of the reduced spreads that have resulted in reduced market-maker profits. As market-maker profits erode, payments for order flow have been reduced and are presently affecting the profit margins of discount and on-line brokerage firms. The consequences to the customers are that those discount and on-line firms that rely on payments for order flow will now have to increase rates or cut their ever-diminishing services. In theory and in fact, brokerage firms will compete for consumers based upon comparison of fully disclosed real commission rates and value-added service.

The brokers who accept payoff for orders violate their fiduciary obligation to you, their client. No one who understands the underlying corruption of payment for order flow would deal with a broker who accepts it. Yet virtually every discount broker accepts these payments in the ordinary course of its business. These payments raise the real cost to you of the trade, in many cases far above the low commission rate you are promised.

It is virtually impossible for any DAET trader to operate a business through a firm that accepts payment for order flow. These firms almost never use SOES for immediate order execution or ECNs for bidding or offering your shares in between the spread. Some even have house rules against it. The discount broker depends on the order flow payoffs to survive, and "best" execution takes a sorry back seat to the broker's own profitability.

Direct Access Electronic Trading makes you a lean, mean trading machine with the tools you need both to make an informed trading decision and to have your order executed in the most cost-effective and efficient manner. I invite you to call your discount broker and ask whether that firm accepts payment for order flow from the broker on the other side of your trade. If the answer is yes, then you cannot trade with that firm because it is working with the other side of the transaction and is more beholden to the other side of the transaction than to you in contravention of its fiduciary duty to you.

WHAT THE NEW ORDER HANDLING RULES MEAN TO YOU

Essentially, the new Order Handling Rules created the basis for equality in the financial markets, with the same rights and privileges for all. Rather than making distinctions between participants as institutional, individual, dealer, market maker, professional, informed, nonprofessional, casual, active, retail, wholesale, inside, outside, informationless, specialists, locals, day traders, international, domestic, and the like, all participants in the market will be considered to be "trading entities." As long as the color of their money is green (or for that matter any color that can be converted into green), they will be welcome to participate on the same terms as everyone else in a fair and equitable manner. While most people would probably agree that this is a wonderful development, there are others whose blood is curdling from these developments.

One of the new SEC Order Handling Rules prohibits market makers from making better bids and offers in Instinet and other secret systems than their bids and offers published on Nasdaq. The adoption of this rule broke forever the stranglehold that Instinet had on the best price. Instinet will no longer be a hidden market you cannot see or access. Second, the SEC requires that limit orders from the public at prices at or in between the spread be displayed on Nasdaq and be available for execution. Thus, any DAET bid and offer in between the spread will become the new best bid or offer. Market makers will have to compete with your DAET bid or offer or let it be executed against. Today, dealers are required to either accept a customer's limit order or ship that limit order to an ECN for display to the entire world.

Under an entirely different new rule, customer limit orders take priority over the market maker's standing. For example, if a market maker is bidding $12\frac{1}{2}$ for a stock and receives a customer limit order at the same price, the customer has standing; and if the market maker buys stock for $12\frac{1}{2}$, the trade would belong to the customer rather than the market maker's trading account. Isn't it a miracle that the customer finally comes first!

Adam Smith spoke of the invisible hand that guides a perfect market. A market is millions of people pursuing their own self-perceived, economic best interests. In a perfect world a perfect market has equal knowledge for all, transparency of best price in all competing markets, and universal, affordable access to the marketplace. That description begins to sound, look, and feel like DAET. A perfect Nasdaq market did not exist because the NASD Trading Committee had deliberately enacted rules and regulations designed to benefit the industry participants to the detriment of the individual investor and trader. The Trading Committee of the NASD was, of course, composed primarily of major market-making firms.

The SEC and the Department of Justice investigations into trading on Nasdaq confirmed that the perfect securities market did not exist. Even in an open outcry market like the futures pit and various commodity markets, the open outcry method of hollering bid and ask prices still allows friends to execute on behalf of each other instead of the public. If the "Solly" broker or the "Goldman" floor trader refuses to recognize a day trading floor broker of the exchange, there is no way for that day trader to trade with the major players. Personal relationships can be dominant in the transaction of any exchange's business unless trading is done impersonally as in DAET/SOES, where buyer and seller only meet on a computer screen—preferably anonymously. The scandals from the commodity pits are too numerous to relate. After trying to corner the silver market, the Hunt brothers learned that bankruptcy isn't all fun and games and sitting around the campfire singing old cowboy and oil dredging songs.

It is very disconcerting to me that we are entering the twenty-first century and major exchanges still allow people to run around yelling at each other or hold scraps of papers in their hands in an antiquated manner hundreds of years old. Paper can get lost or be misread, and open outcry can lead to confusion. I once had an uncle who was severely injured while lugging the stupid end of a piano up a flight of stairs. He shouted to the man on the top end, "Heave *ho!*" The man on the higher stair thought my uncle said, "Leave *go.*" Period.

End of story—Except for the moral that oral and hastily written orders can easily be misinterpreted whereas computerized records are more idiot-proof.

THE INDUSTRY'S TRADING "CONVENTIONS"

The trading system I have described to you had been in place so long that young people who came into the business assumed that these policies were accepted trade courtesies that were not only normal but required. Everyone wanted to believe that practices flowing from these actions were legitimate. Accordingly, concepts like payment for order flow became routine. Exchanging information with each other about orders that the market makers had in hand surfaced as the etiquette of the industry. Traders at the major market-maker houses would routinely espouse to me the "trading etiquette." For example, certain stocks only traded in quarter points and never in eighths—clearly price fixing—demonstrating that market makers had no real understanding of the impropriety they were committing. For the market makers this was business as usual. Corrupt practices had become the concrete binding the structure of the Nasdaq market.

The market makers also were all too willing to blame SOES traders for all negative fallout arising from the ills of the market. According to the market makers, the SOES bandits were responsible for all the problems of Nasdaq and were committing actions equivalent in their minds to destroying the integrity of the market and widening spreads The industry declared open hunting season on SOES traders, who were put on the industry's equivalent of President Nixon's official enemies list.

The market makers packed the important committees and boards of the NASD with people active in or sympathetic to the market makers' interests. For example, even the SEC found that though late trade reporting was common, the NASD maintained surprisingly few records and actively destroyed other records in order to bury the audit trail. The NASD and the market makers continued to blame SOES traders for all of Nasdaq's ills and plotted their downfall.

The Nasdaq economic river was polluted. No one would have predicted that, by 1997, some of the entrenched NASD regulators and top officials would have lost their power and had to leave their jobs in disgrace. Incidentally, officials of such awesome power defy the laws of gravity. Even in disgrace, they never fall down; they fall up and will receive new jobs based upon the contacts they have made.

THE FIGHT FOR POSITIVE CHANGE BEGINS

Perhaps the greatest reward in the world is the sense of accomplishment that occurs when you have achieved your most vivid goal. My dream was to leave a footprint in the history of the markets. Stemming from the early days of my graduate studies, my greatest personal thrill was obtaining insight into the mysterious manner in which the stock market operated, particularly with respect to changes in the market mechanisms. My master's degree thesis was about the impact of Nasdaq on the OTC securities market. As the president of a broker-dealer that had a market-making operation, I had significant exposure to the manner in which the market makers operated and I became aware of the techniques they used when dealing with the public. When I discovered the NASD was allowing its market-maker membership to cheat the public, I became outraged and determined to change the system. It was as if everything I had learned in the past had trained me for this role. I was uniquely positioned to confront the system.

Everyone has a desire to create a worthwhile monument dedicated to change for the best. You want to be able to show your personal creation to your family and proudly say that you have built it for the greater good of other people. This is the self-esteem that warms my heart when I realize that I have

helped to make an honest system out of the Nasdaq market—
a system where the public can have respect for the organic
integrity of prices. Civilization first began when the strong
gave up their right to eat the weak. Today, individuals who
buy or sell stocks will no longer feel that they have been
victimized.

As you might imagine, the odds were against a person
instituting meaningful change in a system as intricate and as
replete with trade customs and usage as the Wall Street
environment. It takes such great effort to change the status
quo that very few were willing to challenge the bureaucracy.
Entrenched financial interests are so powerful that no single
person could fight them. One would think that it was virtually
impossible for one person radically to change a system that
evolved over many years by making accommodations to the
rich and powerful. But they never anticipated the tenacity of a
kid from Brooklyn.

Over the decades substantive and procedural rules, regulations, and trade practices were developed to favor the
industry's interests. In reality these systems and courses of
dealing performed just fine—to the extent that the industry
wanted them to perform in maximizing profits on behalf of
the market makers and guaranteeing order execution firms
maximum payment for order flow. Unfortunately, the public
finished a sorry second, because the industry was able to
benefit from these ingrained practices denied to the public on
a regular basis. Too many people were making extraordinary
sums from the system to have any desire to change it. Those
who clawed their way to the top passed increasingly more
restrictive and self-protective rules to enhance their advantageous position. Effecting change would be like the oil cartel
supporting alternative energy projects.

It took an issue of significant magnitude to give me the
incentive and motivation to fight the NASD and risk everything I owned for change that would benefit my interests as
well as the interests of the investing public. My desire to see
DAET flourish throughout the financial markets compelled
me to risk the time and money, and face attacks on both my

personal character and business, in order to change dramatically the manner in which Wall Street treats your street.

The real issue is to whom do the markets belong and do people have the right to interact in the market without the impediments deemed necessary by the industry? DAET represents public participation in the Nasdaq market in an unfettered fashion. The market makers realized that SOES was the beginning of public intrusion and did everything in their power to eliminate the DAET/SOES encroachment onto their private domain.

This was a classic epic struggle. A David and Goliath fight. A kid from Brooklyn takes on the good old boy, Ivy League, Wharton, Harvard, Princeton rep tie, button down collar, straw hat network. In this corner, weighing 203 pounds (I'm still on a diet), is Harvey Houtkin. In the other corner is the wealth, influence, and power structure of the united elite.

The entrenched defenders always have an advantage over the attackers. The defenders of the status quo use all of their advantages against the newcomers whom they bill as Vandal destroyers of the civilized infrastructure.

When I was fighting with the market makers, I found out why all spiral staircases in old castles were built curving to the right. As the entrenched defenders of the establishment were defending the high ground on the upper stairs, right-handed defenders could lift their swords over their heads for massive downstroke blows while the heathen attackers on the bottom stairs would be blocked from strong sword strokes by the upper ceiling of the spiral staircase. Thus, the infrastructure is usually designed to protect those with already vested interests.

I was the outsider. Right was on my side and I knew that I had to win. As Winston Churchill said, or should have said if he didn't, "In the greatest adversity lies the seed of highest achievement."

My decision to take on the industry with the intent to reform it was not an easy one for me to make. This was the worst time in my life from both a personal and financial perspective. With the collapse of the stock market in the crash of October 1987, I came to the realization that the only way I could hope to day-trade effectively would be through a mechanism that mandated that market makers honor their markets. Depending on the good intentions of the market makers to honor their quoted markets was very naive on my part, bordering on outright stupidity. After a relatively short period of time I realized that getting a proper and timely execution was almost impossible when stocks were moving. Then suddenly it came to me that I was in a position to utilize SOES, which guaranteed immediate execution of orders for up to 1000 shares. This revelation was the shot heard round the world for the beginning of DAET and market equality for all.

Literally from the first day of the implementation of SOES in 1984, I had problems with the NASD over its use to the point where I felt compelled to stop using this apparently wonderful system. In reality no market makers actually used SOES from its inception in 1984 until after the market break in 1988. As a student of Nasdaq, I rediscovered SOES after the crash of 1987 and began to use it quite successfully even in the face of much NASD and industry pressure. The relatively significant economic success I enjoyed by using SOES emboldened me to not buckle under to pressures normally intense enough to bring any small NASD broker-dealer to its knees. The crash of 1987 and the concurrent death of my father drained me of much emotion, including the fear of the NASD and the market makers. These were the circumstances for my decision to go forward.

My small band of SOES electronic day traders were trading exceptionally well to the dismay of the market makers. In the early days of "SOESing," the market makers didn't know how to react to SOES traders. At first, market makers just ignored us. They felt that the powers that be would take care of the SOES "problem" expeditiously. But the trading success continued as more traders used the system.

The immediate problem confronting the market makers was that they refused to accept that SOES activities were becoming mainstream. Rather than making the moves necessary to assure that their quotes were accurate and in line, they just assumed that it would be a short period of time until their regulatory allies would squelch the infidel SOES bandits.

As time passed and SOES continued, the market makers began to lobby their friends at the NASD to enact rules and regulations to put SOES traders out of business. The market makers started the fight and had targeted SOES traders as the enemy, with me as ground zero.

What do you do when a self-regulatory organization like the NASD decides to put your firm out of business? In my case, I had no desire to risk my career for an ideal. Nor did I wish to fight an economic battle with the NASD. It had virtually unlimited funds available, which included even my dues and fees, as well as the securities law of the land to use and interpret as it saw fit. I had been in the industry for 20 years and had been a member of the AMEX, the NYSE, and the NASD; and I had made a significant livelihood in this industry. The NASD's standing threat to anyone who contests the validity or the outcome of their beauty contest is to bar the objector from the securities industry for life. The NASD has the right to sentence the extremist to economic death under its rules because the NASD had been designated a self-regulatory organization with the right to police and regulate the "misconduct" of its members.

Becoming a renegade against the industry in which I had made my living did not come easy. I think the primary motivating factor was the treatment my firm and I received during and after the crash of 1987. I realized then that there was absolutely no camaraderie or spirit of mutual help and concern; the industry was more than happy to sacrifice a few small firms in a rush to maintain the facade of strength and legitimacy of its system. I found it interesting that not one major firm failed in the crash of 1987, which was even more severe than the one in 1929. Apparently, the system worked for the chosen few; the investing public had to rely on the remorseless law of gravity.

THE CRASH OF 1987

SOES was developed by Nasdaq in 1984. Upon its introduction, the NASD and the market makers never expected SOES to be used actively. Its predecessor system, the Order Confirmation Transaction Service System (OCT), was virtually never used in its years of availability despite the fact that it offered tremendous conveniences in communicating orders efficiently and quickly between firms. OCT allowed all firms to communicate orders between each other and execute orders electronically. In reality, an e-mail system like this would have saved millions of dollars in telephone bills alone for the firms that used it and would have assured accuracy for order execution and comparisons, with concomitant staff savings. And yet no one used it! Do you want to know why no one used it? Because Wall Street did not want to relinquish payment for order flow and market-maker accommodations and "conventions." It was far more important to keep the status quo than to save money, become more efficient, and be fair.

The introduction of SOES in 1984 meant very little to the industry because, like OCT, no one expected to use it or to permit anyone else to use it. Even though this system was even better than OCT and delivered instantaneous executions of orders, it made no difference to the industry.

During the next 4 years SOES was hardly used at all (similar to OCT) until the crash of 1987 created a scenario, which turned me from a nice kid from Brooklyn into the *SOES bandit*. The circumstances of the crash in conjunction with my extensive Wall Street background enabled me to take the features of SOES and turn it into perhaps the greatest trading mechanism available since the invention of the telephone. In 1988, the system became a reality.

SOES was established for the immediate execution of orders of 500 shares or fewer. Thereafter, the share limit was raised to 1000 shares of stock. At that time there were no caveats or rules concerning use of SOES. Shortly thereafter the NASD published trading rules that addressed the questions of who could use SOES, how often a person could use

SOES, and *for whom* was SOES use intended. However, these questions were not even a subject of NASD concern in the beginning. The SOES system was just an automatic market execution system to make the execution of small orders more efficient.

The market makers contributed to the crash of 1987, and if not responsible, they certainly exacerbated the collapse by withdrawing their markets from the computer screen. The markets just disappeared. Investors watched in horror as their lifetime savings were melting. Equity vanished as investors couldn't buy or sell any stock position. All they could do was listen to an annoying busy signal on their broker's telephone because the market makers vanished when no market maker wanted to buy in a collapsing market. To the market makers the market disintegration was like the ultimate punch line to the quintessential Wall Street joke, "Sell to whom?"

As the stock market was crashing, market makers abandoned their market-making duties en masse at a time when their support was most needed by the general public. This was a tremendous breach of duty. The market makers disregarded their obligation of making orderly markets in an orderly manner, causing millions and perhaps billions of dollars of losses and a total lack of confidence in the Nasdaq market. This wholesale withdrawal of the orderly market made a sham of the Nasdaq market. Customer confidence eroded as dollars were lost and the market-maker system proved itself to be a cardboard facade.

SOES was expanded after the 1987 crash. The Brady Commission was appointed to investigate the reasons underlying the stock market collapse and to help assure that another crash did not occur. Nasdaq proposed to make SOES participation mandatory for all market makers. Prior to the crash, market makers had voluntarily participated in SOES. Thereafter, if you chose to be a market maker, you had an obligation to honor SOES orders. To prevent a reoccurrence of the 1987 crash, the new rules placed penalties on a market maker's ability to withdraw from a stock.

The rules that followed the Brady Commission recommendations not only mandated the participation in SOES by all market makers, but also increased the market makers' duty to honor their markets. In order to increase market liquidity and the level of investor confidence, the new rules compelled each market maker to increase its SOES participation to five times the minimum SOES obligation size, which in most cases was 1000 shares. If a market maker was offering Apple at 40, that market maker could get SOESed for 1000 shares five times in a row. The Brady Commission felt that this enhanced level of liquidity was necessary to restore the public's confidence in the market.

When SOES became mandatory, more market makers began to feel the obligation to honor their markets. Their markets became electronically real and binding, and the market makers could no longer arbitrarily pick and choose which orders they would honor. The SOES shoe began to pinch. Real, firm, and accessible price quotations ignited the market-maker campaign of public outcry. Electronic execution scared the market makers who were witnessing the beginning of the end of their exclusive way of trading. Needless to say, the market makers, who had been SOESed up to five times simultaneously, were angry. I don't mean that they were slightly upset or moderately concerned. They were becoming embittered. The all-powerful market makers went running for relief to their friends who sat on the Trading Committee of the NASD. Immediately, the NASD made SOES trading its highest concern—a Level 1 priority. SOES, a system designed by the industry to execute small trades efficiently, was in fact strengthened by the crash, was now growing, and ultimately became the catalyst that would irreparably alter the fabric of the market.

I was a real rebel when it came to the old boy system on Wall Street. You can't be warm, fuzzy, and cozy when you represent the forces of change and accountability. The industry wanted to put me out of business because I dared to introduce SOES and computerization to the general public and dared to train John Q. Public in the art of SOES in the attempt to make trading a mainstream occupation.

I had to take a stand because the market makers had nothing to lose except their preferred position, and I had everything to lose. The overwhelming profit potential presented by SOES was a factor significant enough to warrant a fight. I was also compelled by the moral issue of the democratization of trading for the entire public. The NASD, as an industry and as an institution, never wanted the general public actively engaged in electronic day trading. Investing was permitted. Short-term speculation was allowed. The investing public was permitted to live in the suburbs of the stock market but excluded from the second-to-second, minute-to-minute downtown day trading domain where the real action often resided.

The industry was in no hurry to reform its treatment of the investing public because investors rarely demanded change. It was very difficult for an individual to fight for a cause. For one thing, the rewards did not justify the fight. In addition, the adversary, in this case the brokerage industry, was so well financed, and had so much political clout, that even if one chose to fight it, the chances of success would be minimal at best. Moreover, when you consider that the cost of losing the case could include being barred from the industry for life, you can begin to understand the risk I was undertaking. The reward would be Pyrrhic at best because the cost of winning is more than the cost of defeat. In this case, the cost of victory to me was millions of dollars, and the cost of defeat for the normal person would be an eighth ($125) or quarter ($250) of a point on any given trade.

Enter SOES. A system that can and has taken average individuals and turned them into millionaires (also thousandaires), demonstrating that if the Wall Street playing field becomes somewhat level, even an average human being can make amounts of money heretofore never thought possible.

This phenomenon became the impetus for a revolt. When the powers of Wall Street saw that the mechanics of trading were beginning to change, the industry's answer was to rally round its old rules. This time, however, it was different. Now these few dissidents were making enough money where they too could retain competent counsel, petition the courts, and launch a small public relations campaign to champion their cause. The reality is that even if the industry can hire attorneys and pay them a million dollars an hour, it doesn't mean that they will be able to come up with more convincing justification than a $200-an-hour attorney who has morally correct standing. Usually if you have nothing to say, it doesn't matter how much you pay your attorney.

A BRIEF HISTORY OF DAET TIME

I have compiled the following schedule as a brief chronology of relevant events. Note that there have been four significant modifications by the NASD to the SOES rules since 1988, and not surprising, each amendment favored the market makers over the SOES order entry firms. It is very suspicious that officials at the NASD have always voted in favor of the market makers and against you and me.

1963	U.S. congressional study identifies a number of anti-competitive practices in the securities markets, including failing to honor quotations, trading ahead of customer orders, sharing customer and trade information, splitting profits in joint accounts, black-balling other dealers, hiding prices and trades, and keeping spreads wide by agreement among traders.
1984	Nasdaq introduces SOES.
October 1987	The Nasdaq stock market collapses.
1987	The start of investigations concerning the Nasdaq stock market collapse. Recommended changes of the Brady Commission include mandatory SOES participation by market makers with a 5000-share market-maker maximum.
March 1988	I start electronic day trading on SOES.

May 1988   An extensive NASD investigation begins into SOES trading.

August 1988   The first significant NASD amendment to the SOES rules is made. It has the effect of reducing SOES orders by redefining *split orders* to include trades done on a discretionary basis; this rule is interpreted by the NASD to include all trades flowing from a "single investment decision" occurring within a 5-minute period. Also, the NASD enacts a restrictive definition of *professional trader* and adopts the rule prohibiting the use of SOES for a host of customers who were related to the firm's principals including in-laws (the relative rule), each of which was designed to make SOES trading more difficult.

October 1991   The NASD enacts the another group of major modifications to the SOES rules.

1. The NASD expands the professional trading account rules to include any transaction in which SOES is used on any one side of the buy or sell transaction.
2. The NASD adds subjective factors to be considered in determining professional trading account status.

1993   The NASD rescinds the new professional trading account conditions after I sue the SEC in the U.S. Court of Appeals to contest the rules. The court suggests those rules are overly burdensome and vague in the *Timpinaro v. SEC* case.

1993   1. The NASD proposes new Interim SOES Rules until the NASD's proposed N*PROVE System is approved by the SEC. The N*PROVE System, designed by the market makers to replace the SOES automatic execution system, is an inferior order delivery system affording the market makers 20 seconds in which to decide whether to honor their quotes.

2. One of the Interim Rules calls for a reduction in the maximum SOES order from 1000 shares to 500 shares. In addition, the NASD reduces the number of times a market maker can be SOESed from five to two with a 15-second interval between the two executions.
3. Another Interim SOES Rule authorizes Nasdaq to offer an automated quote update feature that would move a market maker's quote away from the inside quote after a SOES execution.
4. Another Interim SOES Rule prohibits short sales on SOES.

December 1993   The SEC approves the Interim SOES Rules as a 1-year pilot project.

January 5, 1994   The Interim SOES Rules become effective on a trial basis.

May 24, 1994   The NASD holds a meeting at Bear Stearns to discuss a draft of the Christie-Schultz study.

May 1994   Domestic Securities (DOMS) begins spread cutting by quoting prices in odd eighths (in violation of the even-eighth convention) and incurs the wrath of the market makers.

May 26, 1994   The Christie-Schultz study is released.

The *Los Angeles Times* reports on the Christie-Schultz study.

May 27, 1994   Several class-action lawsuits are filed against certain market makers, alleging violations of federal and state antitrust and securities statutes.

June 1994   A Department of Justice inquiry into the NASD begins.

Summer 1994   Additional class-action suits are filed.

Fall 1994	The SEC begins a formal inquiry into Nasdaq trading and the NASD.
	More than two dozen class-action complaints are consolidated into one action in the U.S. District Court for the Southern District of New York, alleging an unlawful conspiracy among leading Nasdaq market makers to eliminate odd-eighth quotations in order to increase spreads in violation of the Sherman Act. Earlier allegations of violations of the securities laws are dropped.
December 1994	The NASD tries to extend the Interim SOES Rules.
December 1994	The SEC extends the Interim SOES Rules until March 1995.
November 1994	The NASD forms the Rudman Committee to study and make recommendations on the NASD's structure and governance. The Rudman Committee is not given a charter to investigate Nasdaq.
January 1995	I testify in front of the SEC for a full day; the SEC fails to approve N*PROVE; the NASD is then forced to withdraw N*PROVE.
August 9, 1996	The SEC formally censures the NASD. This is the first time that the SEC had ever censured a major stock market. As the evidence in the SEC/Department of Justice investigations was uncovered, it was obvious that the high-ranking NASD officials knew about the problems and did nothing. This is one of the reasons that the SEC came to the public's rescue.
August 1996	The SEC passes the Order Handling Rules, which establish market transparency and the ECNs.
January 1997	Implementation of the ECNs on Nasdaq.

December 1997   Market makers agree to settle the class-action case
                 for approximately $1 billion.

SOES BANDITS

I never liked the term *SOES bandits.* This was the pejorative name given to us by market makers and NASD officials in order to give us a "bad-guy" connotation. The use of the term *bandit* was a NASD and market-maker attempt to secure SEC approval for regulatory changes curtailing SOES and to prejudice our position in the media by slandering anyone who actively used the SOES electronic execution system. We detested the pejorative "bandit" connotation and the name but did not shy away from it. The term *bandit* had romanticized SOES trading and given us a Robin Hood-like image. Sometimes I felt like a modern-day Zorro, who had assumed the mask of Zorro as a symbol for the DAET community. The industry wanted to give us the same negative image associated with penny stockbrokers, boiler room operators, and other abusers of the public. While firms as notable as Prudential Securities were under investigation relating to the sales of limited partnership interests, Pru continues to do business with an aura of legitimacy as if nothing had happened, but of course, it is one of the boys.

Despite the fact that the activities of SOES traders were 100 percent legal, moral, and correct, we were subjected to negative publicity. Fortunately, America roots for the underdog, and the nickname *bandit* had opened up the door to very helpful public relations with the print and television media. Today, the tide has turned, and many sophisticated thinkers in the financial and regulatory world now recognize that DAET is a true democratization of access to the trading markets. The bad press and negative portrayal of SOES trading has for the most part disappeared and been replaced with more appropriate press coverage of the positive effects of DAET on the spreads, in particular, and the future structure of the markets, in general.

N*PROVE

N*PROVE was a NASD proposed replacement system for SOES. Despite all its advertised features to help the customer, N*PROVE was designed to kill DAET/SOES because it allowed a market maker to avoid its quoted price and back away from a trade with impunity. Market makers always want wiggle room; they would prefer to consider a customer order an option rather than an obligation.

Let me explain the nature of N*PROVE. Market makers never admit that they would use any wiggle room to avoid a trade at their quoted price because it would be illegal as well as unmacho. Wiggle room is any excuse or reason such as "SOES ahead!" (of your trade) for the market makers to avoid consummating an unfavorable trade. They want control over those they trade with and the price at which they trade. I was an SEC subject matter expert on the inner workings of the Nasdaq market. In January 1995 I testified in front of most of the SEC's ranking officials (with the exception of the commissioners themselves). Soon after, N*PROVE promptly disappeared, a situation unprecedented in SEC and NASD history. The N*PROVE system was ultimately withdrawn by the NASD without any formal action by the SEC.

Market-maker thinking is contrary to the way most businesspeople think. Most businesspeople have a retail mentality, where a sales volume of 5000 units is better than 1000 units. The market makers, however, did not want to be forced to trade unless they could preapprove the terms, and orders were considered a put or a call until the market maker could see which way the market would go. An article appeared on August 16, 1993, in *Forbes* magazine entitled "Fun and Games on Nasdaq," describing market-maker practices, including the harassment of traders who narrowed spreads. Notable magazines like *Worth* published articles on collusion and price fixing, but few high-ranking bureaucrats in the NASD read or cared.

Under the 1988 rules that made SOES participation mandatory for market makers, a market maker could be forced to print five fills of 1000 shares at its quoted price. Webster's dictionary would have to come up with new terms to describe market-maker reaction to this phenomenon, and the scale of market-maker displeasure would have to be geometric and not linear. Market-maker outrage on any scale was rising.

The market makers wanted the right to take a second look and be able to walk away before honoring their obligation to trade, if they so chose. The market makers said that the SOES bandits were too fast and took advantage of information that the market makers didn't know. In point of fact, the SOES traders just saw a trend and went with the flow.

Even though Nasdaq was supposed to be a firm market, the market makers naturally wanted to take another look before honoring their price obligations. Come to think of it, so would I. Hindsight is always 20/20 vision. Market makers were anxious to replace SOES with a room-to-maneuver system. The stated purpose of N*PROVE was to replace SOES's *immediate automatic execution* with an *order delivery system.* The proposed N*PROVE system allowed a market maker extra seconds to accept or decline an incoming order before the order was executed by the system.

N*PROVE was a retrograde step with respect to the liberalization of trading. It was a poor concept that the NASD hoped the SEC would rubber-stamp in a business-as-usual manner. The NASD was counting on SEC accommodation.

"SOES AHEAD!"

"SOES *ahead!*" was a common cry at trading houses that wanted to back away from their firm quote obligation, which was to trade at least 1000 shares at their quoted price. There is a double meaning to the term *SOES ahead.* The first meaning is that DAET/SOES trading is leading the markets into the future and is growing every day. The second meaning was an excuse used by market makers to avoid making a trade. *SOES ahead* was an excuse to find a scapegoat. The market maker would say that there was a SOES order ahead of an incoming customer order, allowing the market marker not to trade, even if there was no SOES order.

Market makers used the term *SOES ahead* to avoid execution of an undesirable trade for even a good customer. One time Salomon Brothers, a major and credible market maker, used the *SOES ahead* excuse to back away from a trade when my company called Salomon on the telephone to do a trade because, in fact, the SOES system had been down for 20 minutes. Market makers have told traders I know that an All-Tech SOES order was *ahead* of their order even when All-Tech was not in the market for a particular security.

THE CHANGING SLANT OF THE MEDIA

Initial news coverage inflamed the market makers' story of the activities of the SOES bandits. Newspaper coverage was so slanted in favor of the industry that it was like King John's royal court proclamations reporting on the daily activities of green-clad misfits in Sherwood Forest.

Of course, some reporters may have had a secret agenda. What biased reporters write isn't very interesting because it's predictable and normally going to be wrapping fish a day later. In retrospect, however, it does seem to me that some reporters were returning favors to their friends at various market makers.

Accusing a reporter of being semibiased is like accusing a poker player of being a little bit of a cheat. With full benefit of 20/20 hindsight, I could now feed some words back to a certain reporter who was very sympathetic to the market makers' fables.

If a reporter is investigating a story and goes into it with open eyes, it is not difficult to quickly see who is being forthright and who has something to hide. Fortunately, there are many reporters who do maintain high ethical standards and are not afraid to report the truth as they see it. Many reporters are not puppets of the major brokerage firms and present a fair and unbiased story for their readers.

Not much has changed since the old days. Thomas Jefferson used to say that the most truthful part of a newspaper was the advertisements.

A SECOND LOOK AT THE COST OF COURTESY

The unwritten rule on Wall Street was that if news came out on a stock, a broker had a duty to extend a trading courtesy and tell the contra market maker about the recently reported news. This courtesy also may have violated the broker's fiduciary duty to work for the best interest of the customer. The customer may have been cheated because market makers were more concerned with maintaining their friendly, clublike atmosphere than with a sense of duty to the public. It was simply a case of the order clerk buying favors with your money. Courtesies like this may have cost investors millions and perhaps hundreds of millions of dollars each year.

If news was publically disseminated and the regulators chose to keep the market open, then orders should be handled on a first come, first served basis. Who should have the benefit of information otherwise available to everyone? For example, there are only two known original Mercator projection maps in the entire world. If I find an original Mercator map in an antique store, do I have an obligation to extend the courtesy of sharing my knowledge with the owner?

To sharpen the focus and put the concept into more commercial terms, if I want to buy a snow shovel, do I have to tell the proprietor of the hardware store of a projected storm (giving the proprietor a chance to raise the price) or can I just buy the shovel at its shelf price—especially if news of the storm has already been reported on the radio and television?

THE POWER OF THE ORDER CLERK

On Wall Street, the position of an order clerk is usually considered a relatively modest job. No one studies at the Wharton School of Finance to become an order clerk. However, the order clerk is, in some instances, in a position of tremendous power because trading desks have remarkable latitude concerning how, where, and when orders are executed. This ability to handle orders can put order clerks in an advantageous position to make money for many market makers at the customers' expense. These orders can spell awesome profits to market makers if such orders are handled in a "friendly" manner with respect to the execution time and/or price.

Timing of executions is very important. One telling example occurred to a student in my training program who owned about 4000 shares of Yahoo, which had risen to $42 a share. Our student had not yet opened a DAET account and was trying to sell through conventional brokerage firms without utilizing SOES. He ended up selling half of his stock at $33 and the remainder at $32 a share. Almost 10 points of value had evaporated in the execution process, all in the hands of an order clerk. The moral of this situation is when business is transacted over the telephone, there are no records of when the order is received relative to when the order is executed. Seconds do count.

The order clerks have the latitude to allow the market makers not to honor their market. With DAET, order clerk juggling cannot happen because execution of the trade is automatic and occurs without human intervention. DAET executions tend to be immediate, while e-mail or telephone orders may be delayed upon execution.

The discount brokerage firm can readily ignore a customer complaint and favor the market maker. If you complain, the trading desk wins. The trading desk earns more income each year from the contra-side market maker than you usually generate in commission income to the firm. In the discount brokerage firm's mind, no one has any reason to grumble, especially you. The clerk on the desk is being wined, the clerk's boss is getting payment for order flow, and you as the customer should be grateful because you are paying a discount commission. Everyone should be contented.

Even your friend the broker has no power to challenge the trading desk. If you protest any particular trade or sequence of trades, your broker can offer very little in the way of customer satisfaction, because your broker is more concerned about his or her job. Also, your broker, after passing your order to the trading desk, tends to believe the facts portrayed by the trading desk.

It is difficult to take on an institutional mechanism that has been structured to let you lose. Your broker may be a personal friend but is in no position to help you fight the system. Your broker has no time to conduct a crusade because the phone is ringing with new orders from other customers. It is difficult for a broker to leave a firm. Moreover, after the broker leaves, many "clients" could still be trading with the old firm.

What happens after your friend the broker turns your order to the trading desk? It gets handed to an order clerk. The order clerk now has possession of your checkbook. The order clerk calls the market maker, who may not execute the trade as propitiously as possible because the stock is collapsing, or conversely going up too fast. Later, the market maker may invite the order clerk to dinner. What happened to the broker's obligation to obtain the best price for the customer?

Assume that you've received what you regard as a less than adequate execution. Your only recourse is to go through an arbitration process that takes forever. You are left with the dubious distinction of paying heavy legal fees in a forum where the adjudicator is from the industry that is part of the problem. You get a chance to exhaust your spirit in a grossly inappropriate court of no resort. The industry knows that the customer must submit to arbitration at the NASD. Arbitration is a machine into which you enter a pig and come out a sausage, and it can take years. Even a group as vocal as the SOES traders had trouble challenging the system. The real reason why most people lose in arbitrating a price discrepancy is because there is a rule that requires a customer to mitigate damages. This means that if your broker failed to sell for you at three-quarters, your only damages would be for the next incremental price movement of a quarter because of your duty to mitigate damages. Accordingly, your actual damages may be a quarter of a point, or $250. The industry knows that no sane person is going to hire an attorney and commence an arbitration for $250.

THE OBVIOUS ERROR RULE

The market makers have tried to enforce every available rule against DAET traders. For example, there is an obvious error rule in the industry. If the bid price is 10 and you have erroneously offered to buy at 100 due to a keypunch error, this is an obvious error and the trade will be scratched by agreement of the parties or through NASD intervention.

I had an obvious error in a trade in which the contra party was the trading desk at my own clearinghouse. The trading desk is a separate department from its clearing department. I was on the wrong side of an obvious error, and yet the trader refused to break the trade. He disliked us so he wanted us to suffer the pain of an unnecessary NASD procedure. I called the president of the firm about this discourtesy. The president corrected the problem with a phone call to the trader in a conversation that could have been a career-altering event for the trader.

This event is illustrative of the market-maker mind-set and the manner in which the market makers seemed to seize every opportunity to harrass SOES firms. Even if the SOES firm was correct, the market makers forced the issue and arbitrated whenever possible. They just wanted to make it more difficult for the SOES firms by compelling us to waste time and legal fees in useless endeavors. Pushing SOES firms to arbitration was indicative of the industry attitude that the DAET/SOES traders deserved all of the difficulties the market makers could push their way. They also counted on the NASD to enforce the rules in their favor. Rid the dissenter from the industry, and you rid the industry of the problem.

THE MARKET MAKERS WANTED TO END SOES AND DAET

It is a shock to the market makers that DAET trading is still alive and well.

John L. Watson III, who retired on January 12, 1996, as the president of the Security Traders Association (STA), had championed the fight against SOES and was one of the greatest anti-SOESites in history. In his final remarks to the industry, he acknowledged that the most grievous disappointment of his reign was that SOES was still alive. In his final *President's Report*, dated March–April 1996, he states:

> Our [John seems to speak of himself in the royal first person plural like the Queen of England when she says, "We are not amused," or perhaps he personifies the STA] single largest disappointment was our inability to effect changes to the Nasdaq's Small Order Execution System. We spent more time on this than any other single matter but always came up on the short side. Hopefully in a few months new systems will provide the needed relief to our institution and retail customers and to our firms.

It is inconceivable that the major concern of the market-making industry was the destruction of SOES. After all, we had been in the midst of the greatest bull market in history and market maker profits were at record levels. Think about all the pressing issues involved in the worldwide trading markets. It is irrational and illogical that the main concern of the securities industry was to kill SOES, its own and only efficient order entry system for the small investor.

Look at the market makers' position. The retiring head of the STA claimed that his biggest disappointment was that he couldn't destroy SOES, a NASD-created system that allows any person to execute a maximum 1000-share order. In reality, DAET/SOES trading hit the market makers and the brokerage firms directly in their profit and loss statements. Their respective livelihoods were jeopardized by DAET executions at the best available prices in the most competitive markets. The inability of the industry to verbalize its hatred of DAET/SOES arose because it couldn't tell the truth to the public. While the truth can usually "set you free," in the case of market makers the truth about Nasdaq trading was supposed to be cloaked.

I had a momentous meeting with John L. Watson III at the STA's convention in the fall of 1995 at a cocktail party in Boca Raton, Florida, hosted by Herzog Heine Geduld. It is parenthetically interesting to note that these industry conventions are never held in Jersey City or Bayonne. So then he met me, because I am easy to criticize, easy to deplore, but impossible to avoid. There I was, eating jumbo shrimp as large as Labrador retriever ears. I greeted John L. Watson III with a hearty, "Hi John, how are you."

He showered me with his politician's smile. First and foremost, he was a politician. (Nikita Khrushchev used to say that politicians are the same all over: They promise to build a bridge even where there is no river.) Then he recognized who I was. The original SOES bandit.

We then had a pleasant chat about SOES. My first question was, "What's the problem with SOES?"

His immediate response was that market makers get hit multiple times because of SOES. I explained to him that this was just not possible, and thus not true, because at that time a 15-second delay had been built into SOES between executions. Actually, it was a 20-second delay, but no one knew of the extra 5 seconds that the NASD had stolen for the market makers.

I didn't really want to hurt his feelings, but someone had to tell him. Watson could not verbalize one logical reason why he was against DAET/SOES. He was so caught up in the industry rhetoric that it appeared as though he had never personally thought through the issue for himself.

I proceeded to give him some of the real facts concerning trading in the trenches—a short rendition of the world of DAET/SOES according to Houtkin. Within a few months after this conversation, John L. Watson III tendered his resignation after 11 years at the helm of the STA. I would like to think that I helped to save his soul by confronting him with the truth.

MY COMMENTS ON THE NASD LITIGATION

I am proud to say that the American legal system works. O.J. Simpson discovered that the legal system works well if you have a couple of million dollars to throw at it. It also doesn't hurt to be absolutely correct in your cause and spend thousands of hours agonizing over the legal and moral issues. All you need in order to triumph over a regulatory agency is millions of dollars and devotion to a cause. You should also be willing to lose many hours of your life, and risk the wrath of the bureaucracy and the financial community in which you earn your livelihood. Failure is not a viable option because you could be barred from the industry for life should you lose.

All-Tech eventually prevailed in court. But the out-of-pocket legal and associated costs added up to a seven-digit number. For example, it cost $6000 just to typeset and bind our legal brief in a form the judges on the Federal Court of Appeals would even read. Fortunately, SOES trading was profitable enough for my firm to pay the heavy legal fees and out-of-pocket costs of carrying an otherwise unnecessary litigation.

At the end of the litigation, all the NASD did was rescind a rule that never should have been enacted in the first place. It is difficult to recover money damages from the NASD because it calls itself a quasi-governmental agency. The NASD knows that it has no downside risk in enacting punitive rules. As an investor you paid for the NASD's legal expenses as part of your brokerage commissions.

NYSE MANAGEMENT PRINCIPLES

The absurdity is that top executives of exchanges do nothing to encourage meaningful or helpful change for the betterment of the investors who constitute the ultimate end users of the exchange's services. This do-nothing-at-any-cost policy is pasted to every exchange.

Moreover, the boards of directors are handpicked individuals who owe their success to the system and will tolerate no action that could alter the equilibrium. No director will stand up for accelerated change and risk being dropped from the management reelection slate—with the rare exception when change benefits the industry insiders.

For example, economists have suggested that one cause of the 1987 market break (also called the "Crash" if you lost money) was program trading. Program trading is computerized trading in which, for example, one computer system that is trading index futures snags a low price, which triggers other computerized systems to dump the underlying security. This shark feeding frenzy of continued selling distorts the supply and demand equation, causing the security to drop like Newton's apple due to the influence of artificial selling. The sell-off may start so quickly that there is no time for human intervention, with the devastating consequence that the market fuels its own meltdown.

After the crash, not one major rule change was enacted to prevent continuing programmed trading. A few minor rule changes added meager delays to the timing of when multifarious programmed trading would begin. Once again, the change was to the detriment of the investor.

WHAT YOUR BROKER DOESN'T WANT YOU TO KNOW

OR BEARING THE BULL

REGULATORS ARE POTENTIALLY PART OF THE PROBLEM

A mutually dependent relationship could exist between the regulators of the industry and the brokerage industry which may very well hire these regulators in the future.

Jobs with the regulatory agencies are plums for anyone with a good education who wants to obtain specialized knowledge, make very important contacts in the industry, and be paid to learn. Today's yuppies may spend more time networking than actually working. It is not unheard of for the right people with the right education to get good jobs with the regulatory agencies knowing full well that they will be joining the industry in a relatively short period of time.

Wall Street is a connected industry where everyone with status knows anyone else of potential consequence. I could see where regulators might be tempted to give the industry the benefit of the doubt. Wall Street has a long collective memory. There are no muckrakers in regulatory. Maybe a regulatory job attracts people with a staff mentality instead of people with an innate feeling of being able to make a leadership difference.

THE NASD'S REGULATORY DEFICIENCIES

The SEC staff's investigation of trading on Nasdaq occurred over more than 18 months and included the review of thousands of hours of taped conversations, hundreds of thousands of pages of documents, and the testimony of dozens of market participants and NASD officials and employees. The SEC laid out the evidence and its findings in its *21(a) Report*. This historical portrait may at times seem involved, but it is important to set forth so that we do not have to relive these historic economic issues in Nasdaq or other markets.

Over time considerable acrimony had developed between the market makers and the SOES firms. For example, the SEC interviews with people at SOES firms disclosed that certain market makers frequently made obscene remarks to SOES traders during telephone calls. Review of SelectNet text messages uncovered other harassing messages directed by market makers at SOES firms, although the use of obscenities on SelectNet is prohibited by the NASD. Also, at the 1991 annual meeting of the Security Traders Association, "SOES Sucks" buttons were distributed to general acclaim.

Market makers viewed SOES firms as market professionals who were profiting from rapid-fire trading on a system not designed for such activity. Market makers complained that this activity resulted in their institutional customers receiving inferior prices. For their part, the SOES firms asserted that automatic execution was the best way to complete a trade, because market makers often backed away from the telephone orders placed by SOES firms. Because SOES executions do not require the specific agreement of the market maker to the order, the market makers could not preclude the trading activities of the SOES firms without withdrawing from the market. Market makers turned to the NASD to urge that it limit the impact of SOES.

The NASD became creative by passing new rules and interpreting old ones. My firm was a dues-paying member of

the NASD, and it was unfair for me to have to pay membership dues to an organization that was actively helping my competitors to strangle me. A call went to the finest creative legal
minds of the NASD to write new rules. The NASD answer
seemed quite apparent. Go to the offices at All-Tech and write
down everything Houtkin does during a typical trading day
and make those actions illegal by passing new regulations or
interpreting old regulations to suit the market makers and put
Houtkin out of business. We called these rules the Houtkin
rules, because the objective was to stop Houtkin from using
electronic order execution. If it could stop Houtkin, the
NASD thought the problem would be solved.

Here's the cunning plan. The market makers sought to
deal with the competitive problems posed by SOES by enlist-
ing the support of the NASD in three areas:

1. Rule making and interpretation
2. The aggressive investigation of SOES firms and the
   enforcement of the SOES rules
3. The restriction of NASD admission to SOES firms and an
   increase in conditions for NASD membership

In each of these areas, the SEC found that the NASD took
steps to constrain the activities of SOES firms.

BACKING AWAY

Under the SEC's "firm quote" rule a market maker was
required to execute any order presented to it to buy or sell a
security at a price at least as favorable to the buyer or seller as
the market maker's published bid or offer and up to its published order size. A market maker who failed to meet the firm
quote rule obligations was said to have *backed away* from
its quote. NASD rules also require that market makers honor
their quotations.

The SEC had emphasized that SROs need to enforce strict
compliance with the firm quote rule to ensure that investors
receive best execution and that the market receives reliable

quotation information. As stated in the 88th Congress, 1st Session, Special Study of the Securities Markets, in 1963:

> By quoting ostensibly firm markets over the telephone or wire, dealers represent that a unit of trading can actually be bought or sold at the prices quoted. Upon the basis of these quotations, professionals check competing markets and prices and make their trading decisions. Broker-dealers also obtain these quotations in connection with their retail activities, so that investment decisions of customers and the quality of executions for customers may depend on them. In these and other respects, backing away from quotations impairs a basic mechanism on which orderly operation of over-the-counter markets depends.

Market makers have a fundamental obligation to honor their quotations. Market-maker quotations are one of the foundations of the Nasdaq market and the national market system. The reliability of quotations is essential to investor confidence and to an efficient process of price discovery. Failure to honor quotations deprives investors of the liquidity that market makers advertise they will provide, and diminishes the credibility of the market.

When quotations are not firm, investors seek other means for order execution, which results in market fragmentation. For example, during the course of the investigation, one options market maker informed the staff of the SEC that over the years he had directed approximately 95 percent of his trading in Nasdaq stocks to Instinet and stated that most traders use Instinet because they believe it has better prices and firm quotes. This options market maker stated that Nasdaq quotes are rarely firm and Nasdaq market makers would not display his bids between the inside spread.

The term *backing away* is the heart of the argument in favor of DAET trading. Backing away occurs when a market maker wiggles out of an improvident trade and backs away from a customer order. If market makers honored their market in the first place, there would have been no need for the Brady Commission to have recommended mandatory use of the SOES system to enhance liquidity. In point of fact, SOES was a self-inflicted wound by the financial industry.

Not unexpectedly, the SEC investigation disclosed that a significant number of market makers had failed to comply consistently with their firm quote obligations. Tapes of traders' telephone lines reviewed during the investigation included numerous conversations of market makers declining to transact at their quotes for seemingly spurious reasons. In addition, the tapes of market makers' telephone calls and market makers' testimony disclosed that they often instructed other market makers to "give me ahead," i.e., use the name of the first market maker to claim a trade-ahead exception if a third market maker asked the second to complete a trade. The following is a transcript submitted by the SEC of an audiotaped telephone conversation between two Nasdaq traders at different firms.

Trader 1:   I saw [stock] get a little weaker. I went out and hit [firm 3], and he told me [firm 4] ahead.

Trader 2:   Oh really?

Trader 1:   If [firm 4] comes in to you, give me ahead.

Trader 2:   OK.

Trader 1:   I just don't like the way . . . I don't like the stock. I got a feeling that my seller is going to come back and sell more.

Trader 2:   I got you.

Trader 1:   But I don't want to get you in trouble in the thing, either.

Trader 2:   Oh, it doesn't matter. I made some sales yesterday. I'm long 8 now.

Trader 1:   Yeah. It's that I don't want to see you get hurt, so.

Trader 2:   Look.

Trader 1:   Stay put if you'd like, if you want. And, you know, then give me ahead or tell them you've got me tied up. Why don't we do that? Maybe we'll be able to make some more sales. I'm long about 5.

Trader 2:   OK.

EXCUSED WITHDRAWAL

NASD rules require each member firm to enter and maintain two-sided quotations on a continuous basis for every Nasdaq security in which the member firm is registered as a market maker. The SEC specifically censured the NASD for failure to enforce adequately the mandatory suspension penalties applicable to Nasdaq market makers that did not maintain continuous quotations in accordance with these rules. Under the rules, a member firm that withdrew its quotations in a particular security must also have withdrawn as a market maker in that security for a 20-day period. An exception may have been granted if the market maker obtained excused withdrawal status from the NASD before withdrawing its quote.

Excused withdrawals may have been granted only for the specific reasons enumerated in the rule. In addition, under the rules in the *NASD Manual* a market maker that did not "refresh" its quote in a security within a 5-minute period after its SOES exposure limit had been exhausted would have been deemed to have withdrawn as a market maker in that security for 20 business days (a "SOES withdrawal").

The NASD began routinely to grant waivers for SOES withdrawals for reasons outside the scope of the rules. This practice allowed market makers that failed to refresh their quotes after their SOES exposure was exhausted to avoid the requisite 20-day suspension. Until 1995, the practice of Nasdaq Market Operations was to grant SOES withdrawal waivers as a matter of course without inquiring into the reasons for the withdrawals.

The SEC reviewed a taped conversation between an operations clerk in Nasdaq Market Operations and a trader, which exemplifies this practice.

TRADER: Hey it's [trader's name] from [firm]. How you doing?

CLERK: Alright. Yourself?

TRADER: Good and not so good. I got suspended in Apple. The trader's assistant's out and we're a little short on the desk, I'm calling from [firm name].

CLERK: [firm symbol]?

TRADER: Yeah.

CLERK: Okay, I'll put you back in.

TRADER: And I'm, I'm going to update it so it's, so it's a greater amount.

CLERK: [unclear] See, the thing is not what you're doing as far as upping. The thing is, somebody's got to watch out, because . . . the thing is, we're not supposed to be doing this.

TRADER: Right, Right.

The SEC investigation revealed that a market maker merely had to request the waiver and Nasdaq Market Operations granted it. The SEC found that market makers were granted waivers after their SOES exposure had been exhausted because they were away from their desk, working another order, or covering another trader's stocks. None of these was a reason listed in the applicable rules. The NASD lack of enforcement of the unexcused withdrawal rule undermined a fundamental premise of the dealer market: that market makers stand willing to buy and sell securities at all times. Allowing market makers to evade this responsibility reduced liquidity in the market and threatened the ability of investors to execute trades.

NASD HARASSMENT

The NASD made enforcement of the SOES rules a priority. Planning documents of the NASD district offices expressly identified "aggressive enforcement of SOES rules" as a goal, and various Market Surveillance Department staff members devoted substantial time and effort to enforcement of the SOES rules.

Complaints made by market makers to other individuals at the NASD were also passed on to Market Surveillance for possible review. Senior Nasdaq officers ensured that Market Surveillance followed up on the complaints of market makers. Market makers lobbied the NASD to take disciplinary action against SOES activists. An April 1995 memo from the NASD Liaison Committee of the STA reads:

> There is considerable consternation in the Street over what is perceived as the NASD's inability to discipline "SOES firms" for obvious violations of the Short Sale Rule. The senior staff of Market Surveillance, the Chairman of the Market Surveillance

Committee and the NASD President have been informed of
this growing resentment. Look for the NASD to take some
severe action in the near future or else face a difficult situation
with its market makers.

In a 1992 memorandum, a senior NASD executive wrote
that the market makers are:

extremely frustrated and angry. Unless they get some immediate relief the subject of SOES abuse is going to come back to
haunt us.

One "possible measure" identified in that memorandum
was:

immediate prosecution of SOES violations with simultaneous
suspension from SOES. I can't emphasize how important this
is. Even if we bring a precise, abbreviated complaint that can
get immediate relief, following up with a full investigation with
all i's dotted and t's crossed.

The NASD made substantial efforts to identify the SOES
firms and closely monitor their trading activity. SOES firms
were generally subjected to routine examination every year
even though they shouldn't have been. Routine examinations
were conducted on 1-, 2-, or 3-year cycles, depending on how
the firms were classified. Firms were categorized as Level 1, 2,
or 3 on the basis of various characteristics of the firm and its
business. The lower the level, the more frequent the examination. SOES firms, along with other types of firms such as
penny stockbrokers, were considered Level 1 firms that must
be examined every year.

Just to put this in proper focus, you should understand
that Richard Ketchum, the chief operating officer of the
NASD, had been quoted in the *New York Times* describing
SOES as the most "honest" way to execute a transaction.

The NASD staff used the lists to identify firms for which
special SOES "sweep" exams were conducted. The SOES
sweep examinations in January 1991, for example, were
scheduled to coincide with the beginning of the Persian Gulf
war because the NASD staff believed that the commencement
of hostilities might result in a severe market downturn.

Examiners from District 10 in New York City were dispatched to five SOES firms described in a NASD memorandum as "potential SOES rules violators" to look for improper short-sale violations. Although the examinations did not uncover any breach of the SOES rules, the exam report discussed the trading habits of SOES firms.

In one instance, the NASD instituted an accelerated enforcement proceeding against a SOES firm. A senior NASD enforcement officer sent a congratulatory letter to the Market Surveillance Department staff members who worked on this proceeding which stated that:

> there is *no better service quality we could have provided to our market maker customers* and the individual investor. (Emphasis added.)

This emergency remedial proceeding was only one of two such proceedings ever brought by the NASD. But even more importantly, how dare the NASD refer to the market makers as "our . . . customers."

PROFESSIONAL TRADING ACCOUNTS

The whole issue of professional trading accounts was ludicrous from its inception. The Market Surveillance Department did not have objectively defined benchmarks or guidelines with which to determine if an account was a professional trading account (PTA). In its release approving the amendment of the PTA rule, the SEC addressed the issue of the generality of the rule by stating that:

> while the NASD will have discretion to determine exactly what is "excessive" and to determine based upon these factors which accounts are professional trading accounts, the NASD is required to act fairly and reasonably.

The facts uncovered in the SEC's investigation indicated that this discretion appears not to have been properly exercised.

The NASD made itself the sole judge of what constituted a professional account. It gave itself the power to declare you a professional if it deemed a pattern of SOES trading to exist. Of course, there were no definitions of what constituted a "pattern." In one instance, an account was declared a professional when that person averaged less than one round-trip a day on SOES.

The NASD never conducted any studies or had empirical evidence to justify any of these restrictions to SOES. The NASD never articulated any rational need or basis for declaring anyone a professional account or excluding a professional account from the market. These rules were issued under the interpretive powers of the NASD.

The NASD did not publish any guidelines specifying what frequency of short-term trades or short-sale trades was "excessive." Even the NASD analysts and supervisors responsible for selecting accounts for possible PTA designation did not have objective criteria for distinguishing between excessive and acceptable trading. Contemporaneous notes and testimony concerning a June 27, 1990, meeting of the Trading Committee indicated that the committee believed that excessive trading should not be defined quantitatively and a "you know it when you see it" standard should be used.

I challenged the amendments to the PTA definition as being overly burdensome and vague, and the PTA rule was ultimately repealed after being criticized by the U.S. Court of Appeals for the D.C. Circuit in *Timpinaro v. SEC* [2 F.3d 453 (D.C. Cir. 1993)].

Bill Timpinaro was a plumber and the quintessential nonprofessional trader. The senseless part of the professional trading account rules was that they literally applied to the account and not the trader. The NASD would deem the account a professional account but nothing prevented the trader from opening another account and continuing to trade. I knew that I had won the litigation when a court of appeals judge asked whether there was a restriction on the number of accounts you could have. The SEC vacillated on an answer to the judge, perhaps because the SEC disagreed with the NASD on the issue of whether the account or the trader became a professional. The same judge then replied that the issue in the case was really about electronic account opening and not electronic trading. Then a second judge asked why it was legal for Paine Webber to have electronic access but not the plumber.

In retrospect, I would say that the SEC experiences in *Timpinaro* and the withdrawal of the PTA rule was the turning point of the DAET/SOES legacy.

SELECTIVE REFUSAL TO TRADE

Certain market makers have backed away from orders presented to them by firms that the market makers "disliked" or perceived to be overly competitive. Some market makers preferred not to trade with firms that they considered to be "professional traders," such as SOES firms. The evidence before the SEC indicated that some market makers wanted to avoid trading with such firms because the trading styles of such firms may have left market makers at a disadvantage. For instance, some market makers had testified that they believed that these firms would "front-run" market makers' orders or "pick off" market makers who were slow to update their quotes following news announcements. In this context, the term *front running* is used to describe a practice of entering orders immediately after learning information that could affect the market for a given security. Such practices between market makers are considered unprofessional or unethical and are discouraged within the market-maker community.

The SEC found that the selective refusal of certain market makers to trade with these firms further eroded the underpinnings of the firm quote rule, and was unfair and inconsistent with the concept of a free and open market. It also hindered the development of the national market system. The firm quote rule was weakened if market makers could pick and choose the parties with whom they would trade. Refusals to trade contributed to market fragmentation, and thereby impaired pricing efficiency and fairness to investors.

THE PRICING CONVENTION

Before late May 1994, the pricing convention was widely followed by Nasdaq market makers. According to testimony from Nasdaq traders, the convention was based on tradition and represented the "professional" way to trade in the Nasdaq market. Market makers expected other market makers to follow the convention. Several traders testified that senior traders at their respective firms trained them to follow the pricing convention. Still other traders admitted to following a practice of setting quote increments based on the size of the dealer spread, but stopped short of characterizing the practice as a "convention." In their testimony before the SEC, traders had also described the practice as an "ethic," a "custom," or a "tradition."

Under the pricing convention, stocks with a dealer spread of $\frac{3}{4}$ or more were to be quoted in even eighths (even-eighth stocks). More than 80 percent of all domestic Nasdaq national market stocks, of which there were more than 3200, followed the pricing convention. Nasdaq national market stocks (also referred to as "NMS stocks") were the top tier of Nasdaq stocks in terms of capitalization, number of shareholders, and activity. These companies comprised over 95 percent of the capitalization of all Nasdaq companies.

The SEC noted that natural economic forces did not explain the absence of odd-eighth quote combinations, but such an absence would be expected under the pricing convention.

THE ROLE OF INSTINET

Although adherence to the pricing convention acted to prevent market makers from displaying odd-eighth quotes for even-eighth stocks on Nasdaq, it did not keep them from entering odd-eighth bids and offers for those same stocks on alternative market systems such as Instinet and SelectNet. Instinet does not accept retail customers. Because Instinet expresses market makers' willingness to deal at stated prices, such orders may be regarded as the functional equivalent of market-maker quotes. SelectNet is an electronic trading system owned and operated by the Nasdaq Stock Market, Inc., and is available as a trading vehicle only to NASD member firms. Instinet Corporation is a wholly owned subsidiary of Reuters International.

Market makers regularly placed orders to buy or sell even-eighth stocks at odd-eighth prices on these systems, while quoting the same stocks almost exclusively in even-eighth increments on Nasdaq. One tape obtained by the SEC in its investigation contained a conversation by a market maker who refused to put an odd-eighth quote on Nasdaq when requested to do so by a retail broker, but indicated he would put an order on Instinet containing the odd-eighth quote. He explains to the broker that displaying an odd-eighth quote in the stock on Nasdaq would make a "Chinese market," which was considered unprofessional and which other market makers did not like. He stated:

> I really can't do that 'cause it creates what they call a Chinese market, stock trades in $\frac{1}{4}$ point. I'm on Instinet. If somebody wants to whack me at $\frac{7}{8}$ths, that's where they're going to whack me.

Only certain brokers, market makers, and institutional investors had access to the quote information and trade opportunities displayed on Instinet and SelectNet. They were not directly available to individual investors and other market participants. In the following conversation, taped by the SEC, two traders commented upon a suggestion made at a meeting by another trader (Trader 3), who proposed that retail customers be given access to Instinet:

TRADER 1: What did he [Trader 3] have to say?

TRADER 2: "I come from [firm], and we do a lot of retail, and I think there ought to be a way that our customers have access to Instinet." I'm like,

TRADER 1: What?

TRADER 2: What?

TRADER 1:   Well, then you wouldn't do the retail, you moron.

TRADER 2:   Like [name of Trader 3], then there'd be no need for you, you jarhead.

The advantages to market makers of such limited access systems fostered the development of a two-tiered market—the public Nasdaq market for retail investors and some institutional investors and the private, limited-access systems where broker-dealers and certain large institutional investors could observe and trade at better prices, yet in similarly sized trades, as in Nasdaq. The availability of these systems, particularly Instinet, reduced the necessity to narrow the Nasdaq spreads, thereby facilitating adherence to the pricing convention and reducing competition in the Nasdaq market. One trader's testimony before the SEC illustrated this point:

> Back in the eighties you really did not have Instinet as it was [sic] today and so sometimes you would move your market up, you would close your spread to try to signal to another market maker hey, in this case, say going up in the bid I am a buyer and you might go twenty-nine and an eighth bid and stay there for a while and then go down to let people know you are a twenty-nine and an eighth buyer. You have tried institutional and you cannot find. Instinet was not what it was [sic] today; they did not do that kind of volume, so the only way to really let the world know you are a buying [sic] rather than just take them the twenty-nine and a quarter stock is to close your spread or do what you call the odd eighth.

THE CHINESE MARKET

Various Nasdaq market makers had exerted pressure on other market makers who acted inconsistently with the trading conventions (by narrowing the inside spread and consequently reducing the profits of all other market makers in the stock). The SEC investigation developed evidence of instances where market makers like my firm, Domestic, entered quotes that narrowed the inside spread and then were the subject of harassing telephone calls. These badgering calls came from other market makers questioning or complaining about the narrower spread. They demanded that the spread cutter widen the spread back out, asserting that the spread reducer was ruining the market or was unprofessional, unethical, embarrassing, or guilty of "making a Chinese market."

At times, a degree of imagination was applied to the harassing telephone calls. When Domestic narrowed the spread on certain occasions from a quarter to an eighth, it received anonymous telephone calls in which the caller, in a phony Chinese accent, ordered chop suey, moo goo gai pan, or other Chinese food, in an apparent allusion to the understanding among market makers not to make "Chinese markets." Spread-shortening market makers also reported to the SEC instances where other market makers expressed their displeasure by disseminating messages over the SelectNet system. In addition to delivering orders, SelectNet can be used to transmit short text messages. Examples of messages complaining about spreads included "Ridiculous," "Great Market," "Stop kidding," "How about 64s," and "Not Funny."

In addition, spread-narrowing makers who had the audacity to maintain a truly competitive market by violating the conventions encountered vicious refusals by other market makers to trade with them. It is difficult to make a living by trading if no one will trade with you.

While these examples of harassment and intimidation were documented by reporters or disclosed on the many hours of tapes reviewed by the SEC and the Department of Justice, the real situation was far more intense than the examples reported. Intimidation was a daily occurrence that eventually became comic relief at my office because we knew the perpetrators were no more than frustrated armchair warriors. Even though the threats didn't really phase me, the failure of market makers to observe their obligations and trade ethically and honorably was most disturbing. For alleged leaders in the financial community to act in such a juvenile and undignified manner was unbecoming. These actions diminished any remaining respect that I still might have had for the industry and further convinced me that my quest to initiate reform was correct.

THE BEAR STEARNS MEETING AND SUBSEQUENT NARROWINGS

In the spring of 1994, market makers began to narrow spreads in a number of high-profile stocks. Several events appear to have precipitated this development.

On May 24, 1994, the Security Traders Association (the STA) sponsored a meeting to discuss the width of spreads at the Manhattan offices of Bear Stearns (this became known as the "Bear Stearns meeting"). The STA, a trade association composed of individuals in the securities industry, largely represents the interests of market makers. The meeting was attended by approximately one hundred traders from many of the major Nasdaq market-making firms, as well as senior officers of the STA and the NASD. The president of the STA began the meeting by urging traders to narrow spreads voluntarily or face regulations forcing a tightening of spreads.

In his prepared remarks the STA president prophetically announced:

> [L]et me suggest that if we do not voluntary (*sic*)
> close . . . quotes, it will be done by regulation by the NASD, the
> SEC or Congress and in the meantime we will lose many companies to the exchange (NYSE) and receive much bad and distressing publicity.

He also quoted from the Christie-Schultz study and from a letter from an issuer complaining about the Nasdaq spread.

NASD senior officers then made a presentation showing that the spreads of top Nasdaq securities had widened and that in many stocks the displayed spread was substantially wider than the spread at which the stock actually could be traded.

PUBLICATION OF THE CHRISTIE-SCHULTZ STUDY

On May 26, 1994, several major newspapers reported that the Christie-Schultz study had concluded that market makers tacitly colluded to maintain wide spreads. The NASD had received a draft of the Christie-Schultz study in late 1993 and was concerned about its conclusions. Some market makers became aware of the study in early 1994 before the study had been widely publicized. These concerns appeared to have prompted certain market makers to reduce the spreads of several high-profile Nasdaq stocks beginning in late May 1996. In several taped telephone conversations, traders attributed the narrowing of the dealer spreads in late May to the Bear Stearns meeting and the reports of the Christie-Schultz study conclusions.

On October 19, 1994, reports of a Department of Justice investigation into allegations of price fixing by Nasdaq dealers were published. The following day, the *Los Angeles Times* began a six-part series highly critical of the Nasdaq market. The article was written by Scott Paltrow and entitled "Inside Nasdaq, Questions about America's Busiest Stock Market." The *Los Angeles Times* series was critical of the Nasdaq market and described instances of harassment of my market-making firm, Domestic, which had narrowed spreads.

Scott Paltrow became a major catalyst. Scott spent several hours delving into my perception of the industrywide abuses of the public. Apparently after researching and verifying the facts, he proceeded to write a revealing article. I applaud Scott's courage and viewed this as one of journalism's finer moments.

The first article identified a trader at one market-making firm (Firm A) which called Domestic and complained, "You guys break the spread for 1,000 shares?" The next day, Firm A began to move its quotes in $\frac{1}{8}$ increments.

The NASD decided to investigate these incidents. Domestic had previously complained to the NASD's Market Surveillance Department about at least one of these incidents. Domestic sent a letter to the Market Surveillance Department on June 6, 1994, describing the episode and attaching a printout of a harassing SelectNet message. According to Domestic's letter, a market maker sent the message "Pathetic" to Domestic immediately after Domestic had narrowed the inside spread in Intel from a quarter to an eighth. NASD records confirm this sequence of events.

The Market Surveillance Department sent a form letter to the market maker in question, asking for its explanation for sending the "Pathetic" message. The market maker responded by letter on June 20, 1994, asserting that when its trader observed Domestic's tightening of the spread, he tried to trade with Domestic. The letter stated that when Domestic refused to enter into a trade, the trader transmitted the "Pathetic" message to Domestic. A review of the NASD's own equity audit trail revealed that Domestic, in fact, purchased 1000 shares of Intel from the market maker. The NASD closed the matter without further investigation.

It was only after the *Los Angeles Times* article was published that the NASD revived the investigation. According to the *Los Angeles Times*, market makers made the following comments to Domestic:

1. "You guys break the spread for 1,000 shares?"
2. "You're embarrassing and pathetic. . . . You're breaking spreads for everybody,"
3. "This is ********. I have institutional customers who come to me and I have to match your price. It's ********, you guys going down an eighth for a thousand shares."

In November 1994, the staff of the Market Surveillance Department spoke to the three market makers involved in the incidents noted in the articles. All three market makers denied that any statements they made to Domestic were in retaliation for its breaking the spread. Instead, the traders attributed any disparaging remarks to Domestic's refusal to trade for more than 1000 shares. There was a widely observed but wholly illegal and anticompetitive industry custom of not initiating a new inside bid or offer unless the market maker was willing to trade in large size (at least 2000 to 5000 shares), even though the NASD firm quote rule only called for market makers to be willing to trade 1000 shares, at the most.

In the end, the Compliance Subcommittee recommended that a letter of warning, which was the lightest sanction available, be sent to one market maker. The subcommittee distinguished between the fact that the "Pathetic" message was sent on SelectNet, while the other two comments were made over the telephone. The NASD staff indicated that this fact was not a meaningful basis for distinction, but failed to convince the subcommittee to change its recommendation. After similar discussion at the Market Surveillance Committee the next day, the letter of warning was issued and the other matters dismissed.

THE SO-CALLED AUDIT TRAIL

During the course of its investigation, the SEC staff encountered significant difficulties reconstructing trading activity in the Nasdaq market. Broker-dealer order tickets, among the most fundamental of records, were too often unavailable or inconvenient to retrieve. Time stamping was often unreliable for the purposes of determining compliance with applicable rules, such as the firm quote rule and limit order protection rules. At one firm, the time stamping did not include seconds, which particularly frustrated the SEC's ability to reconstruct the market.

A further difficulty was the inadequate documentation of telephone orders received at OTC trading desks. As noted above, order tickets, if they were available at all, were not always reliably time-stamped.

As a result of the SEC investigation, the NASD has begun to design and implement an audit trail sufficient to reconstruct markets promptly, monitor them effectively, and enforce its rules.

COORDINATED ACTIVITY AMONG MARKET MAKERS

The evidence uncovered by the SEC indicated that instead of dealing as competitors at arm's length, certain Nasdaq market makers had coordinated particular trade and quote activities with one another, furthering their proprietary interests at the expense of investors and other market participants. This coordinated conduct had included:

1. Arrangements under which these market makers agreed to move their published quotes at the request of other market makers, or assist one another in executing trades.

2. Agreements to delay reporting specific trades likely to have a negative impact on the value of the requesting market maker's trading position or to obscure the true sequence of trades from customers or other market participants.

3. The routine sharing of information by these market makers concerning customer orders, securities positions, trading strategies, and intended quote movements. Although many market makers attempted to coordinate their activities on a widespread basis, such coordination was particularly pronounced among market makers that had regular and close contact in the course of trading the same securities. When testifying before the SEC, some traders had referred to these cooperative traders as "friendly competitors."

DELAYED REPORTING OF TRADES

The SEC uncovered instances in which some market makers entered into explicit agreements to delay reporting trades. The following transcript from the SEC report is an example of market makers' agreeing to delay a print to hide it from a customer.

TRADER 1: I just sold 25 at $\frac{1}{4}$, $\frac{1}{8}$ for any part of whatever you want.

TRADER 2: Oh, that's ******* beautiful, buddy.

TRADER 1: . . . .

TRADER 2: Why don't I sell you—This sounds so horrible—I'm gonna sell you, is 10 G's okay? . . .

TRADER 1: . . . .

TRADER 2: . . . I'd love to sell you 10, I owe you one.

TRADER 1:   I bought 10 at $\frac{1}{8}$, and don't print it for, for a few minutes, 'cause I told the guy I'm just making a sale out of the blue. Alright?

TRADER 2:   I'll, I'll print after the bell.

TRADER 1:   Thanks, bud.

THE RETURN TRADE COURTESY

If additional orders were received from the customer, the market maker with the order also considered itself under a "professional" obligation to seek to trade first with the market maker with whom it last traded. It was also generally understood that a market maker that hit another market maker's bid or lifted its offer would not thereafter move its quotes without first consulting the market maker with whom it had just traded.

IMPROPER DISCLOSURE OF CUSTOMER ORDERS

Market makers who failed to disclose their customers' orders were considered "unprofessional," at times received complaints and harassing phone calls from other market makers, and risked losing access to information and trading opportunities provided by others. For example, in one taped conversation, a trader complained to another trader who did not fully disclose his customer's order when they first traded:

TRADER 1:   . . . if you had more you should just show me your picture. I try and make good prints for you. But—

TRADER 2:   . . . I'm dealing with a very difficult customer. I ask him, "How much have you got to sell?" . . . They don't even— they say, "**** you. I ain't telling what's for sale. This is what I've got. Work it."

TRADER 1:   Ok.

TRADER 2:   That's how it's done—I mean, I'm not playing games. Believe me. I'm the last person in the street to play those things.

TRADER 1:   Ok, I was, it's just that, I mean I got long the stock trying to move it with my retail when you offer it down. And I don't have any room to pay out the credit to my broker. Then I get stuck, stuck long 10. You offer it down. Then I end up having to go out and hit the stock. And I mean it's not doing anybody any good. . . .

TRADER 2:   Alright . . . I hear you.

TRADER 1:   Just . . . I understand with these guys you can't communicate with them. But if in the future, if you'd like to try, think it would make us both a lot more money.

Trader 1 later complained to a trader at another firm about Trader 2: "You know, we try to do the right thing. We keep an orderly market. And this guy just ****** all over us."

In this situation, Trader 1's desire to keep the quotes from dropping while making retail sales was inconsistent with the interests of the customers to whom his firm was selling stock.

THE COURTESY OF MUTUAL COOPERATION

Market makers relied on each other to provide order flow, information, and cooperation to help them trade positions profitably. In one taped conversation, two traders discussed the benefits of sharing information and cooperating:

TRADER 1:   . . . you've bailed me out a couple of times too. That's the game.

TRADER 2:   Yep.

TRADER 1:   You know? And, uh—

TRADER 2:   And by you helping me out in some of these other ones. I mean, I'll always make you money in the Vicor [VICR] that, you know, anytime you get a position and stuff like that. That's, you know, that's nice that way.

TRADER 1:   Help each other. I'm more than, even if I have to lose a lot of jake [money]. I don't care.

TRADER 2:   Yeah.

TRADER 1:   Because, bottom line is everything comes out.

TRADER 2:   Well, it makes my life a ****-of-a lot easier knowing that you can tell me what's going on when I got some things going, you know—Like the other times I got something going on in something so I can just tell you. And just tell you to get the **** out of the way.

Traders did not want other market makers to perceive them as being "uncooperative," "unethical," or "unprofessional" because that perception could have resulted in their losing access to their trader networks. Market makers would refrain from sharing information with or offering trading opportunities to those market makers who failed to comply with the "professional" trading practices discussed herein. Exclusion of market makers who did not follow these practices served to deter competition in the Nasdaq market.

AFTERWORD

In sum, the SEC found that the pricing convention, the size convention, the disincentive against narrowing the spread, the attendant enforcement mechanisms, and the availability of nonpublic trading systems for market makers resulted in a fragmented market for Nasdaq stocks. Moreover, the SEC concluded that investors were often confronted by artificially wide, inflexible spreads, and frequently could not transact in the markets at the best prices. Attempts by dissident market makers to compete on the basis of price were in a number of instances met with hostility and harassment.

Operating a stock market is a sacred public trust. This trust was undermined by the activities of the market makers who ruled the NASD's important committees and the directors and officials at the NASD.

I have told you what your broker won't tell you. You have eaten from the tree of knowledge and are no longer the "informationless" customer the industry wants you to be. The DAET Garden of Eden still exists and you are welcome to enjoy all its bounty. If you are enticed, you may continue your further education in many ways as you cast your votes for greater investor and trading prosperity by using DAET for further personal gain.

DAET is the story of a struggle against the privileged few who were in a position to benefit from the market environment. The public was the only winner in the battle to implement positive change on Nasdaq. No decorations or awards were given to me, to the traders of my firm, or to All-Tech.

DAET stands for equality based upon merit in which every qualified DAET trader could join the first-class trading club

without running the gauntlet of a blackball or other discriminatory practice. We are talking about leveling the playing field,
with equal opportunity for all regardless of race, religion,
creed, age, gender, or any other barrier to entry.

Secrets of the SOES Bandit has revealed the motivations
hidden in markets by divulging the concealed agendas of the
financial industry. These same secret agendas exist in other
markets, and I will not rest until the NYSE is an electronic
market where you and I can have an electronic seat.

Even though Mark Twain warned against making predictions, "especially about the future," the electronic trading
markets of tomorrow will be forged link by link as a result of
what you and I do today.

Harvey Houtkin
David Waldman

You can e-mail the authors at:
harvey@attain.com   or davidw@attain.com

NASDAQ GLOSSARY

The Nasdaq stock market lists over 5000 domestic and foreign companies, more companies than any other stock market in the world. In 1995, Nasdaq share volume surpassed that of all other U.S. stock markets.

What distinguishes Nasdaq is its use of computers and a vast telecommunications network to create an electronic trading system that allows market participants to meet over the computer rather than face-to-face. The other major distinguishing feature is Nasdaq's use of multiple market makers. On Nasdaq the typical stock has 11 market makers actively competing with one another for investor order flow.

American Depositary Receipt (ADR) A security, created by a U.S. bank, that evidences ownership of a specified number of shares of a foreign security held in a depositary in the issuing company's country of domicile. The certificate, transfer, and settlement practices for ADRs are identical to those for U.S. securities. U.S. investors often prefer ADRs to direct purchase of foreign shares because of the ready availability of price information, lower transaction costs, and timely dividend distribution.

Ask The quoted offer at which a market maker is willing to sell a stock. (See also *Best ask*.)

Best ask The lowest quoted offer of all competing market makers to sell a particular stock at any given time.

Best bid The highest quoted bid of all competing market makers to buy a particular stock at any given time.

Bid The quoted bid at which a market maker is willing to buy a stock. (See also *Best bid*.)

Deleted A security no longer included in the Nasdaq stock market.

Electronic Data Gathering, Analysis, and Retrieval (EDGAR)   An electronic system implemented by the SEC that is used by companies to transmit all documents required to be filed with the SEC in relation to corporate offerings and ongoing disclosure obligations. EDGAR became fully operational in mid-1995.

Foreign   A non-U.S. company with securities trading on the Nasdaq stock market.

Held   A situation where a security is temporarily not available for trading (e.g., market makers are not allowed to display quotes).

Inside market   The highest-bid and the lowest-offer prices among all competing market makers in a Nasdaq security, i.e., the best bid and offer prices.

Last-sale reporting   An electronic entry by NASD members to the Nasdaq stock market of the price and the number of shares involved in a transaction in a Nasdaq security. The trade must be reported to Nasdaq within 90 seconds of the execution of the trade.

Long position   Ownership of a security, giving the investor the right to transfer ownership to someone else by sale, the right to receive any income paid by the security, and the right to any profits or losses as the security's value changes.

Market maker spread   The difference between the price at which a market maker is willing to buy a security and the price at which the firm is willing to sell it—i.e., the difference between a market maker's bid and ask for a given security. Since each market maker positions itself to either buy or sell inventory at any time, individual market-maker spreads are not indicative of the market as a whole. (See also *Inside market*.)

Market makers   The NASD member firms that buy and sell Nasdaq securities, at prices they display in Nasdaq, for their own account. More than 500 member firms act as Nasdaq market makers. One of the major differences between the Nasdaq stock market and other major markets in the United States is Nasdaq's structure of competing market makers. Each market maker competes for customer order flow by displaying buy and sell quotations for a guaranteed number of shares. Once an order is received, the market maker will immediately purchase for or sell from its own inventory, or seek the other side of the trade until it is executed, often in a matter of seconds.

Market Surveillance   The department responsible for investigating and preventing abusive, manipulative, or illegal trading practices on the Nasdaq stock market. Considerable resources are devoted to surveilling the Nasdaq stock market. A vast array of sophisticated automated systems reviews each trade and price quotation on an on-line, real-time basis. Off-line computer-based analyses are conducted to evaluate trading patterns on a monthly, weekly, and daily basis.

Whenever any of these automated systems indicate unusual price or volume in a stock, Nasdaq Market Surveillance analysts determine if this was the result of legitimate market forces or perhaps a violation of rules. Among other things, analysts review press releases, look at historical trading activity, and interview brokers, market makers, and Nasdaq-listed company officials. Market Surveillance continues its inquiries until unusual movements are adequately explained.

If legitimate market forces were at work, the case is closed without action. If it appears rule violations have occurred, a disciplinary action is initiated. When corporate insiders or members of the investing public are involved in a potential violation, the case will be referred to the SEC.

Material news   News released by a Nasdaq company that might reasonably be expected to affect the value of a company's securities or influence investors' decisions. Material news includes information regarding corporate events of an unusual and nonrecurring nature, news of tender offers, unusually good or bad earnings reports, and a stock split or stock dividend. (See also *Trading halt.*)

Momentum   The rate of acceleration of an economic, price, or volume movement. An economy with strong growth that is likely to continue is said to have a lot of momentum. In the stock market, technical analysts study stock momentum by charting price and volume trends. What goes up, however, must come down.

Most active   The most active Nasdaq national market stocks.

Nasdaq International Ltd.   A subsidiary of the NASD headquartered in London, England. Its mission is to support NASD members in London, serve as a liaison to international companies seeking to list securities on Nasdaq, encourage foreign institutional participation in Nasdaq stocks, and heighten the international image of the NASD and its markets.

Nasdaq International Service   An extension to the Nasdaq stock market's trading systems that allows early morning trading from 3:30 to 9:00 a.m. EST on each U.S. trading day. This Nasdaq service enables participants to monitor trades during London market hours. NASD members are eligible to participate in this session through their U.S. trading facilities or through those of an approved U.K. affiliate.

Nasdaq national market securities   The Nasdaq national market consists of over 3000 companies that have a national or international shareholder base, have applied for listing, meet stringent financial requirements, and agree to specific corporate governance standards. To list initially, companies are required to have significant net tangible assets or operating income, a minimum public float of 500,000 shares, at least 400 shareholders, and a bid price of at least $5. The Nasdaq national market operates from 9:30 a.m. to 4:00 p.m. EST, with extended trading in SelectNet from 8:00 a.m. to 9:30 a.m. EST and from 4:00 p.m. to 5:15 p.m. EST.

Nasdaq small-cap market securities   The Nasdaq small-cap market consists of over 1400 companies that want the sponsorship of market makers, have applied for listing, and meet specific and financial requirements. Once a company is approved and listed on this market, market makers are able to quote and trade the company's securities through a sophisticated electronic trading and surveillance system. The Nasdaq small-cap market operates from 9:30 a.m. to 4:00 p.m. EST, with extended trading in SelectNet from 8:00 a.m. to 9:30 a.m. EST and from 4:00 p.m. to 5:15 p.m. EST.

National Association of Securities Dealers, Inc. (NASD)   The self-regulatory organization of the securities industry responsible for the regulation of the Nasdaq stock market and the over-the-counter markets. The NASD operates under the authority granted it by the 1938 Maloney Act Amendment to the Securities Exchange Act of 1934.

Net change   The difference between today's last trade and the previous day's last trade.

No quote (NQ)   No market makers making an inside market at this time.

Open order   An order to buy or sell a security that remains in effect until it is either canceled by the customer or executed.

Penalty bid   A syndicate penalty bid can be displayed on the Nasdaq system during the period of a registered public offering of a security. Such a bid may be entered by the managing underwriter or a member of the underwriting group acting on its behalf, and is intended to facilitate the offering by stabilizing the price of the security during the distribution period. This activity is permissible under SEC Rule 10b-7.

Presyndicate bid   A presyndicate bid can be entered in the Nasdaq system to stabilize the price of a Nasdaq security prior to the effective date of a registered secondary offering. This activity is permissible under SEC Rule 10b- 7.

Previous day's close   The previous trading day's last reported trade. The previous day's close on the Nasdaq web site is updated at 8:30 a.m. EST.

Principal orders   Refers to activity by a broker-dealer when buying or selling for its own account and risk.

Real-time trade reporting   A requirement imposed on market makers (and in some instances, non-market makers) to report each trade immediately after completion of the transaction. Stocks traded on the Nasdaq stock market are subject to real-time trade reporting within 90 seconds of execution.

Securities and Exchange Commission (SEC)   The federal agency created by the Securities Exchange Act of 1934 to administer that act and the Securities Act of 1933. The statutes administered by the SEC are designed to promote full public disclosure and protect the investing public against fraudulent and manipulative practices in the securities markets. Generally, most issues of securities offered in interstate commerce or through the mails must be registered with the SEC.

Short interest   The total number of shares of a security that have been sold short (see *Short selling*) by customers and securities firms.

Short positions   Stock shares that an individual has sold short and has not covered as of a particular date.

Short-sale rule   The Securities and Exchange Commission rule requiring that short sales be made only in a rising market; also called *plus tick rule*. A short sale can be transacted only under one of these two conditions: (1) if the last sale was at a higher price than the sale preceding it (called an *uptick* or *plus tick*), or (2) if the last sale price is the same as the preceding sale which was an uptick (called a *zero-plus tick*). The short-sale rule was designed to prevent abuses perpetuated by so-called pool operators, who would drive down the price of a stock by heavy short selling and then pick up the shares for a large profit.

Short selling   The selling of a security that the seller does not own, or any sale that is completed by the delivery of a security borrowed by the seller. Short selling is a legitimate trading strategy. Short sellers assume the risk that they will be able to buy the stock at a more favorable price than the price at which they sold short.

Sale of a security not owned by the seller: A technique used (1) to take advantage of an anticipated decline in the price or (2) to protect a profit in a *long position*.

An investor borrows stock certificates for delivery at the time of a short sale. If the seller can buy that stock later at a lower price, a profit results; if the price rises, however, a loss results.

An investor borrows stock certificates for delivery at the time of short sale. If the seller can buy that stock later at a lower price, a profit results; if the price rises, however, a loss results. A commodity sold short represents a promise to deliver the commodity at a set price on a future date. Most commodity short sales are *covered* before the *delivery date*.

Example of a short sale involving stock: An investor, anticipating a decline in the price of XYZ shares, instructs his or her broker to sell short 100 XYZ, which is trading at $50. The broker then loans the investor 100 shares of XYZ, using either its own inventory, shares in the *margin account* of another customer, or shares borrowed from another broker. These shares are used to make settlement with the buying broker within five days of the short-sale transaction, and the proceeds are used to secure the loan. The investor now has what is known as a *short position*—that is, he or she still does not own the 100 XYZ shares and, at some point, must buy the shares to repay the lending broker. If the market price of XYZ drops to $40, the investor can buy the shares for $4000, repay the lending broker and thus cover the short sale, and claim a profit of $1000, or $10 a share.

Short selling is regulated by Regulation T of the Federal Reserve Board. The Nasdaq Short Sale Rule prohibits NASD members from selling a Nasdaq national market stock at or below the inside best bid when that price is lower than the previous inside best bid in that stock.

Spread   The spread for a company's stock in influenced by a number of factors, including:

Supply or "float"

The total number of shares outstanding available to trade

Demand or interest in a stock

Total trading activity in the stock

Stock symbol   A unique four- or five-letter symbol assigned to a Nasdaq security. If a fifth letter appears, it identifies the issues as other than a single issue of common stock or capital stock. A list of fifth-letter identifiers and a description of what each represents follows:

A	Class A
B	Class B
C	Issuer qualifications exceptions (This indicates that the issuer has been granted a continuance in Nasdaq under an exception to the qualification standards for a limited period.)
D	New
E	Delinquent in required filings with the SEC
G	First convertible bond
H	Second convertible bond, same company
I	Third convertible bond, same company
J	Voting
K	Nonvoting
L	Miscellaneous situations, such as depositary receipts, stubs, additional warrants, and units
M	Fourth preferred, same company
N	Third preferred, same company
O	Second preferred, same company
P	First preferred, same company
Q	Bankruptcy proceedings
R	Rights

S   Shares of beneficial interest

T   With warrants or with rights

U   Units

V   When issued and when distributed

W   Warrants

Y   ADR (American Depositary Receipt)

Z   Miscellaneous situations such as depositary receipts, stubs, additional warrants, and units

Syndicate bid A bid that can be entered in the Nasdaq system to stabilize the price of a Nasdaq security prior to the effective date of a registered secondary offering. This activity is permissible under SEC Rule 10b-7.

Today's high The intraday high trading price.

Today's low The intraday low trading price.

Trading halt The temporary suspension of trading in a Nasdaq security, usually for 30 minutes, while material news from the issuer is being disseminated over the news wires. A trading halt gives all investors equal opportunity to evaluate the news and make buy, sell, or hold decisions on that basis. A trading halt may also be imposed for purely regulatory reasons, by either the Nasdaq stock market or the SEC.

INDEX

INDEX

ABOUT THE AUTHORS

HARVEY HOUTKIN, the original "SOES Bandit," is chairman and CEO of All-Tech Investment Group, Inc. Houtkin's decade-long utilization of Nasdaq's SOES system for electronic day trading laid the foundation for today's electronic trading revolution. He has been quoted and/or written about in numerous periodicals including *Time, Forbes, Fortune, BusinessWeek*, the *Wall Street Journal*, and the *London Financial Times*, and appears regularly on television and at seminars.

DAVID WALDMAN is a senior vice preseident of All-Tech. An accomplished author and praticing attorney for over 30 years, Mr. Waldman was a member of the New York Futures Exchange, where he originally learned how to trade.

Questions may be addressed to
Harvey@attain.com
David@attain.com